The Last Seven Months
of
ANNE FRANK

Pantheon Books
New York

The Last Seven Months
of
ANNE FRANK

Translated from Dutch by
Alison Meersschaert

Willy Lindwer

Library of Congress Cataloging-in-Publication Data
Lindwer, Willy.
    [Anne Frank. English]
    The last seven months of Anne Frank / Willy Lindwer.
      p.   cm.
    Translation of: Anne Frank.
    ISBN 0-679-40145-8
    1. Frank, Anne, 1929–1945. 2. Holocaust, Jewish (1939–1945)—
Netherlands—Personal narratives. 3. Holocaust survivors—
Netherlands—Interviews. 4. Netherlands—Ethnic relations.
I. Title.
DS135.N6F734413 1991
940.53'18'0922—dc20
[B]   90-53437

Book Design by Karin Batten
Manufactured in the United States of America
First American Edition

*With special gratitude to the women who
contributed in such a remarkable way to the creation
of the documentary film and this book.*

*For my grandmother Rivka, who was murdered in
Poland by the Nazis.*

Contents

Preface

This book contains the complete interviews conducted for my film documentary *The Last Seven Months of Anne Frank.* The film was first televised in May 1988 in the Netherlands. Since then it has been shown in many other countries all over the world, including the United States in 1989. In the course of my work on the documentary, I found that only a small portion of each interview could be used in the film, although every interview contained material of sufficient importance to be preserved in its entirety. Thus this book not only supplements and rounds out the film, but it is, above all, a historical record of the admirable courage of the women who recount their dramatic experiences here.

The research and preparation for the film took more than two years, and many preliminary conversations were necessary before the interviews could be recorded. In recounting their experiences, the women underwent great emotional and psychological stress; yet the need to tell their stories prevailed.

Through the filmed interviews, an attempt is made to reconstruct a period during the Second World War. The six women all knew Anne Frank in the last seven months of her life, and although they tell of their own experiences, many aspects of their stories also reflect the story of Anne Frank.

I developed a special bond of friendship and trust with each of these women. My admiration for their enormous strength is difficult to express. Through this work I have come to better understand the burden that each of them—and all who survived the horrors of the German concentration camps—bears.

Although I belong to the postwar generation, I come from a Jewish family that suffered heavily during the war. Therefore the material was not unfamiliar to me. And yet, these interviews with survivors from Auschwitz made it clearer than ever to me what it meant to be deprived of one's freedom and to be subjected to the horrors of the German extermination camps.

Of those who participated in this project, I owe special thanks to A. H. Paape, Director of the Royal Institute for War Documentation in Amsterdam and Renée Sanders, free-lance journalist and coworker on this project. I should also like to express my gratitude to Bob Bremer, program director at TROS television in the Netherlands, who helped the project along with his active interest and support.

I am grateful to Elfriede Frank and the Anne Frank Foundation in Basel, Switzerland, for their sympathetic support. In particular I want to thank my wife, Hanna, who supported me at critically important moments and made substantial contributions to both the film and the book.

Amstelveen, July 12, 1988   Willy Lindwer

Introduction

Anne Frank has become the best known symbol for the murdered Jews of the Second World War. Her diary, which she wrote between June 12, 1942 and August 1, 1944, while she was in hiding in the "Annex," was published in more than fifty countries. It has been the inspiration for many stage, screen, and television presentations.

The Annex itself is now a museum and has attracted hundreds of thousands of visitors from all over the world.

It was inevitable that the picture which emerged from the diary would become romanticized by a large public, especially the generation born after the war—many of whom have read the adventures she began to record in her diary during one of the most tragic periods in our history. She was thirteen at the time, fifteen when she died.

On Tuesday, August 1, 1944, Anne wrote the last letter to her diary. On August 4 the SD (the German Security Service) raided the Annex at No. 263 Prinsengracht. All those who were in hiding there were arrested. Anne's own writing ends here.

Arrest, deportation, and annihilation are the final unwritten chapters of Anne's diary and of six million Jewish victims, of whom more than half were women and children. From the moment of arrest, Anne's life-in-hiding in the Annex, the letters to her diary, the romantic and idealized notions of a young girl give way to the harsh, ruthless reality of the Nazi concentration camps, where unprecedented genocide was committed. Here Anne, her sister Margot, and their mother Edith met their deaths.

Over the years, relatively little attention has been paid to Anne's life following her arrest and deportation. There was no extensive research, and in some cases the meager sources contradicted each other. Thus almost nothing was known about the final, fateful seven months of her life, or how she endured the bitter misery in Westerbork and Auschwitz-Birkenau. She died of disease, starvation, and exhaustion in Bergen-Belsen in March 1945—a few weeks before the liberation.

More than forty years later, only a few people are left who are able and willing to tell about that time. The women who survived and whom I interviewed were unable at first to talk about their experiences. To this day, several still can't. Gradually some have found the words—as the process of assimilating the Holocaust continues for them. Some feel a need for catharsis, others want to tell their stories for posterity. They know they are among the last eyewitnesses to these unreal and incomprehensible times in human history.

In the film, and in this book, women speak—women who, like Anne, were in Westerbork, Auschwitz-Birkenau, and Bergen-Belsen. They describe what happened on the transports and in the camps where Anne stayed.

The women knew Anne and her family. Several had even gone to school with her or were friends of hers. Because the interviews are complete, the book fills in the background and milieu of each of these women and, as a consequence, places them in the context of a much broader contemporary picture.

Some differences exist in the accounts and viewpoints of some of the details of Anne's final seven months. Perhaps the exact historical facts are less important than a record of what Anne and these women—who approached the limits of human endurance—went through.

They tell about their fear of death and how facing the deaths of others day in and day out forced them, for the sake of their own survival, to hold their own feelings in check. Above all they tell about the small human details which played such a big role in the camps where there were no longer any norms.

After many months of research, with the help of the State Institute for War Documentation, we succeeded in finding women who were prepared to talk before the camera and microphone about their personal experiences in the German concentration camps. All had shared experiences with Anne Frank and her family after their arrest. These women experienced a deep personal pain, which each has endured in her own way and coped with, or perhaps is still trying to cope with—a pain from which no one can ever really recover. Their personal stories and their views of what happened are an important contribution to our understanding of that traumatic period of history. Anne Frank shared these experiences. The women speak for her.

These reports are *needed.* Fascism, Neo-Nazism, racial discrimination, and anti-Semitism still exist today. Even the authenticity of the diary has been questioned. For these reasons most of the witnesses were ready to tell their stories. They wanted to bring the injury inflicted upon them out into the open and thus perhaps to combat injustice wherever it exists.

It is worth noting that the voices we hear are those of women. The horrors inflicted on women and children by the Nazis have received relatively little attention up to now. Their testimony proves all the more clearly that Nazi insanity knew no bounds. The book recounts the feelings of women in a time of severe hardships. Human beings were being degraded to the level of animals. Every human sensibility and all standards were swept away. That these women survived can be considered a miracle: Auschwitz and Bergen-Belsen were not designed for survival.

These brave women will carry an immense burden all their lives. That they chose to share their experiences is a demonstration of courage for which we can all be grateful.

HISTORICAL
OVERVIEW

Historical Overview

In 1933, Otto Frank decided to leave Frankfurt, a city with a large Jewish community, and to emigrate to Amsterdam. He foresaw that Hitler's rise to power boded disaster for the Jews.

The Frank family—Anne, born June 12, 1929, her sister Margot, who was three years older, and their mother and father—lived in Amsterdam at 37 Merwederplein. There, as the daughter of well-to-do parents, Anne spent carefree years. But the Nazi invasion of the Netherlands in May 1940 cast a shadow on this happy childhood, and the situation became worse with the increasing restrictions placed on the Jews. Among these was the regulation that Jewish children were permitted to attend only Jewish schools.

Nevertheless, Anne had a relatively pleasant time, marked by a busy social life at the Jewish Lyceum (a school established by the German occupiers under the auspices of the Amsterdam Jewish Council). Edith and Otto Frank did everything in their power to protect their daughters as long as possible from the increasing pressure of the occupation.

However, in July 1942, Margot received a summons to report for work in the "East." For Otto Frank this was sufficient reason to go into hiding with his family. The Franks were relatively fortunate. They knew people like Miep and Jan Gies and others who were ready to help those in hiding. This was unusual; most Jews did not have such contacts.

A second exceptional point is that the Frank family remained together during the entire period they were in hiding. Most of the families of the 25,000 Jews hiding throughout the Netherlands were separated.

With the help of employees of his firm, Otto Frank had made thorough preparations in an annex that was located be-

3

hind the business premises. The Franks were to be joined at 263 Prinsengracht by their friends, the Van Daans and the dentist, Dussel, at this building—the offices, work rooms, and warehouse of the German firm Opekta, founded by Otto Frank in 1933. The firm produced pectin, used in making jams and jellies.

At the beginning of July 1942 the Frank family went into hiding. In the diary which Anne had received as a present for her thirteenth birthday a few weeks earlier, she describes this time in great detail: the circumstances and the feelings of a young girl growing up, her relationship with her parents and her sister, and the tensions that developed among those who were hiding in the Annex. Her first letter to her diary was dated June 12, 1942.

The final entry was made on August 1, 1944. Three days later, the German police and their Dutch assistants, under the command of Karl Silberbauer of the SD (Security Service), arrived at the door of the Annex. All the occupants and two of those who had helped them were taken by truck to the SD headquarters on Euterpestraat.

The day after their arrest the Frank family was transferred to the Huis van Bewaring, a prison on Weteringschans. On August 8, they were transported from the main railroad station in Amsterdam to the Westerbork detention camp.

From the time the Nazis first began to round up Jews in the Netherlands in the summer of 1942, Westerbork in Drente had been used as a transit camp, a part of the deportation apparatus which funneled Jews to various German concentration camps. Westerbork was guarded by Dutch regular police and military police. In the period between the summer of 1942 and the fall of 1944, eighty-five trains left Westerbork for the extermination camps, nineteen of these went to Sobibor and sixty-six to Auschwitz.

For a month the Franks were kept in the "disciplinary" barracks (barracks 67), not as ordinary prisoners, but inmates convicted of a crime, because they had not reported for deportation, but had been arrested while in hiding. On September 3, 1944, aboard the last transport to leave the Netherlands, Anne Frank, her family, and their comrades-in-hiding were brought to the Auschwitz-Birkenau extermination camp. By then more than 100,000 Dutch Jews had been deported. This last transport to Auschwitz consisted of 498 men, 442 women, and 79 children—a total of 1,019 people.

Barely 120 miles separated the transport from the Allied forces who by this time had already reached Brussels.

The transport arrived in Auschwitz during the night of September 5. Almost immediately after its arrival men and women were separated. The following day, 549 people from this last transport, among them all the children under fifteen years of age, were sent to the gas chambers of Auschwitz-Birkenau. Women who had not been selected for extinction had to walk to the Birkenau women's camp. Among them were Edith Frank and her daughters.

With gruesome precision a horrifying mass murder was being carried out in Auschwitz-Birkenau, the largest Nazi death camp. Its goal: the total extermination of entire peoples such as Jews and Gypsies. It was mass murder which in organization and scope has no comparison in world history.

By September 1944 almost two million people, the majority of them Jews, had been gassed in Auschwitz-Birkenau.

After the arrival of the last transport from Westerbork, there were about 39,000 people in the women's camp. Edith Frank and her daughters, Margot and Anne, landed in Barracks 29.

Margot and Anne stayed in Auschwitz-Birkenau almost two months, some of this time in the so-called *Krätzeblock,* the "scabies-barracks," since both had *Krätze* (scabies). Because Mrs. Frank didn't want to leave her daughters, she stayed with them until both girls were shipped to Bergen-Belsen, probably on October 28, 1944. On January 6, 1945 Mrs. Frank died in Auschwitz-Birkenau of grief and exhaustion.

By the end of October 1944 the Russians were about 60 miles from Auschwitz. From that time on, many women were transported from Birkenau to other concentration camps. Some were taken to the work camp at Libau, where they were assigned to the factories supplying the German war machine.

Anne and Margot were sent to Bergen-Belsen on October 28. Originally Bergen-Belsen had been one of the "better" camps; it had at first served as an "exchange camp" *(Austausch-lager)* for Jews who were to be exchanged for Germans detained outside Nazi-controlled territory. But during the final months of the war, living conditions in this camp, which was in a barren part of the Lünenburg Heath, were so bad that, although there were no gas chambers, ten thousand people died.

Toward the end of 1944, numerous barracks had been added to one of the worst sections of the camp, the so-called *Sternlager* or "Star Barracks"—a reference to the yellow star the inmates had to wear—and the situation in the camp became much worse. There was almost nothing to eat, it was winter, and sickness and disease were everywhere. Conditions deteriorated even more with the arrival of several transports, especially those from Auschwitz at the end of October and beginning of November 1944.

As the Allied forces approached and the end of the war neared, the Germans no longer knew what to do with the many concentration camp prisoners. Masses of people were jammed into Bergen-Belsen, which had not been designed to accommodate such large numbers. The new barracks, especially in the women's camp, were not yet ready, and in great haste a tent camp was set up for the women who had come from Auschwitz-Birkenau. Among them were Margot and Anne Frank. One week after their arrival, several of the tents were swept away by a severe storm. The overcrowding of the camp soared during the winter months; the miserable living conditions deteriorated even further. As as result, in the last months before the liberation of Bergen-Belsen and in the first weeks thereafter, most of the inmates perished. Among them were Margot and Anne Frank, who died of typhus within days of each other. The camp was liberated by the British shortly after, on April 15, 1945.

In 1953 the Dutch Red Cross reported that of the 1,019 people on the transport that left Westerbork on September 3, 1944 for Auschwitz, 45 men and 82 women survived.

HANNAH ELISABETH PICK-GOSLAR

"Lies Goosens"

Hannah Pick-Goslar

S*everal telephone conversations preceded our first meeting in December 1987, in Amsterdam. Hannah Pick-Goslar, who with her younger sister survived Bergen-Belsen, emigrated to Israel after the war, with the help of Anne Frank's father, Otto.*

As I imagined, she was a likeable, cheerful, and talkative woman, down-to-earth and unemotional. After forty years she still spoke Dutch fairly well. When I suggested that we return to the place where she had last seen her closest childhood friend, Anne Frank, she did not hesitate for a moment. She would go. Her son Chagi, who didn't want his mother to return to Bergen-Belsen alone, accompanied her. One of three children, Chagi is a great help to her.

The story of Hannah's life is a perfect reflection of the history of Jews during the twentieth century. She and her parents fled Nazi Germany in 1933 for the Netherlands. Hannah survived the horrors of Bergen-Belsen and settled in Israel, the dream of Theodor Herzl, whose Zionist ideas she and her family admired. Chagi, a Sabra born in Israel, is a scientist, and an officer in the Israeli army. This visit to Europe was his first.

Hannah Pick appears a number of times in Anne Frank's diary under the pseudonym "Lies Goosens." (Otto Frank changed the names of the people mentioned in the diary when it was published.) Before filming the documentary, we visited various places which she and Anne had known in their childhood. In many ways, Hannah's and Anne's early years were quite similar. They were both four years old when they fled Germany in 1933 for the Netherlands. They were neighbors on the Merwedeplein in the southern part of Amsterdam, and grew up together there. They went through kindergarten, elementary school, and high school together, right up to the moment when the Frank family went into hiding in July 1942. They did not see each other again until early in 1945 when, shortly before Anne's death, they spoke together several times across the barbed wire of Bergen-Belsen.

11

Hannah Elisabeth Pick-Goslar

"Lies Goosens"

I was born into an observant Jewish family in Berlin in 1928. My mother, Ruth Judith Klee, daughter of a well known Berlin lawyer, was a teacher. My father, Hans Goslar, was deputy minister for domestic affairs and press secretary of the Prussian cabinet in Berlin. Even before Hitler came to power, he saw which way the wind was blowing, and we began to prepare for our flight to the Netherlands.

In Holland, my father, a professional economist, opened a small office with another refugee, a lawyer named Ledermann. They provided legal and financial advice to refugees. It was not a lucrative enterprise, but my father earned a living. In 1933, we moved to the Merwedeplein in Amsterdam.

In Germany, my father had been one of the founders of the Mizrachi, a religious Zionist organization. Every four years, he attended the Zionist congresses, so my father knew the Dutch members of the Mizrachi well. I believe that these people helped us. My father made friends quickly; and he was respected in Jewish circles. We had no direct contact with people outside of the Jewish community.

How I got to know Anne Frank is very interesting. In the very first week after our arrival in Amsterdam, I went with our maid—also a refugee—to a store to buy butter and milk. We met another maid there who was also a refugee and didn't speak Dutch either. The two maids started talking and it turned out that another refugee family lived on our side of the street, at number 37 on the Merwedeplein. We lived kitty-corner below them in number 31. The next day we met the Frank family.

There were two daughters—Margot, who was three years older than I was, and Anne, who was half a year younger than I was. My parents and Mr. and Mrs. Frank very soon became friends, although they were from very different backgrounds. Mr. Frank was a businessman. Mrs. Frank, I believe, didn't have a profession. In contrast to my parents, the Franks weren't religious at all. Both of my parents had an academic background.

They became very close friends, partly because of the language, but also because we were in the same situation. Both families, after all, had been forced to leave Germany and to live in the Netherlands as refugees.

Mr. Frank was an optimistic person. When he entered a room, the sun began to shine. He was always in a good mood. My father, on the other hand, was more of a pessimist. Ultimately, my father was right, but it was much more pleasant to hear what Mr. Frank had to say.

Every Friday evening the Frank family came to visit us, and we also celebrated Passover together at our house. Every year, for the Feast of Tabernacles, Sukkoth; we would build a tabernacle in the small walkway between the yards on Merwedeplein and the Zuideramstellaan. The tabernacle was very small because it was so narrow there. Anne, of course, often came to look at it, and sometimes she stayed to eat with us. She may also have helped decorate the tabernacle.

On Yom Kippur, the Day of Atonement, we fasted the entire day. Mr. Frank and Anne would stay home to prepare the evening meal, while Mrs. Frank and Margot went to the synagogue just like my parents. When I was still a little girl—you didn't have to fast until you were twelve years old—I was always sent to eat with the Frank family. Then my mother could go to the synagogue without worrying about me. Mrs. Frank and Margot went to the synagogue once in a while, but Anne and her father went much less frequently.

At Anne's house they celebrated *Sinterklaas* (the Dutch feast-day for Saint Nicholas on December fifth). We didn't at my house, because we only observed the Jewish holidays. We celebrated Hannukah. At school I could, of course, participate; there was always a party at school on the day after *Sinterklaas*—a play, or something like that.

The fact that I was then an only child, and that the Frank family had a daughter who was my age also helped our friendship. I thought it was wonderful to go to their house. Anne and I, of course, also went to the same kindergarten. I can still remember the first day. My mother brought me to school. I couldn't speak Dutch yet, and my mother was very anxious, how it would turn out, how I would react. But when I went in, there was Anne standing across from the door, ringing the bells. She turned around and I flew into her arms, and my mother was able to go home reassured. I had dropped my shyness and forgotten my mother in the same instant.

After kindergarten, we attended the same school for six years, the Sixth Public Montessori School, which is now named the Anne Frank School. Later, we went to the Jewish high school together—more about that later.

I never went to school on Saturdays, since we were observant religious. Orthodox Jews don't go to school on Saturday—the Sabbath. Anne did. And every Sunday, she would come to my house, or I would go to hers, to do our homework.

Quite often on Sundays, we would go with her father to his large office on the Prinsengracht—now the Anne Frank

House—and we would play there. I didn't see the Annex then. There was a telephone in every room, and this gave us the chance to play our favorite game: telephoning from one room to another. That was quite an adventure. And we played a lot of street games. We also played tricks on people. On the Merwedeplein we'd throw water out of the window onto the people walking by.

I can still remember that we once played *Voetje van de vloer* (a Dutch children's game, like hopscotch), and when we got home, we heard a report on the radio that there had been an earthquake somewhere. We laughed a lot about that!

Because I was getting a religious education and Anne wasn't we didn't always have the same days off. On Wednesday afternoons and Sunday mornings, I had to study Hebrew. Margot also took Hebrew lessons, but Anne didn't. She followed in her father's footsteps and wasn't religious at all.

Anne's parents always came to our house on the Jewish holidays, and at other times, such as New Year's Eve, we would go to theirs. Then we were allowed to sleep together in her room. At midnight, they would wake us up, and then we would get an *oliebolletje* (a jelly doughnut) and something to drink. The day after New Year's was a holiday, and we could sleep late. That was always a lot of fun, staying with each other, like a special party.

When we went on vacation in the summer, we took Anne with us. Anne hung a photograph of our little vacation house above her bed, the same photograph as in her room in the Anne Frank House. Anne must have liked it very much otherwise she wouldn't have chosen this picture to hang up. When we went to Zandvoort for a day in the summertime, we would ask Mrs. Frank if Anne and Margot could go with us. They were just like sisters—my mother and Mrs. Frank.

We made a group of three friends—Anne, Hanne, and Sanne, but Sanne went to a different school. And then there was another girl who was my Sabbath friend. She went to the Jeker School. Every Saturday I met her in the synagogue and played with her in the afternoon. Anne was a little jealous about this friend; as she wrote in her diary (much later) on November 27, 1943, that she had dreamed about me and asked why she, Anne, lived, and I, Lies, had died—she thought that I was dead. She also wrote that it had been very mean of her to want to take my friend away from me, and how I might have felt. Naturally, we also had arguments, but we were very normal girls, so that was to be expected. But generally we were very good friends and always talked things over and played together.

Anne loved autograph books in which everyone had to write a verse. She had a lot of friends. I think she had more boys as friends than girls, especially when she was in the sixth grade and then in the first year at the Lyceum. Boys really liked her. And she always liked it a lot when all the boys paid attention to her.

She was always busy with her hair. She had long hair and she was always fussing with it. Her hair kept her busy all the time.

She also had a special funny trick that I had never seen before. Whenever she wanted to, she could move her shoulder out of its socket. She thought that it was great fun to have the other children watch and burst out laughing.

Anne was a sickly girl. I don't know what the problem was, because she almost never had a high fever, but she often stayed home in bed. That would last a couple of days. She probably had rheumatic fever. I would always visit her then and bring the homework assignments to her. But she was always very cheerful. She loved little secrets and she loved to chat. And she collected pictures of movie stars, which you can still see on the walls of the Anne Frank House. Deanna Durbin and some others. I was never very interested in that. But both of us collected pictures of the children in the royal families of the Netherlands and England. We traded for those. And she began to write. She was always game for a prank.

She was a stubborn girl. She was very good-looking. Every-

16

one generally liked her, and she was always the center of attention at our parties. She was also the center of attention at school. She liked being important—that isn't a bad quality. I remember that my mother, who liked her very much, used to say, "God knows everything, but Anne knows everything better."

Anne was given a diary on her thirteenth birthday. There was a party in the afternoon and we saw that she had gotten a very beautiful diary from her parents. I don't know if it was the first or second one that she had, because I remember that Anne was always writing in her diary, shielding it with her hand, even at school during the break. Everybody could see that she was writing. But no one was allowed to see what she had written. And I thought that she was writing entire books. I was always very curious to know what was in the diary, but she never showed it to anyone.

I never could find out what was in it, but I have thought that there must have been much more than there was in the published diary. Maybe they never found all that she wrote before she went into hiding—she had already been writing for a couple of years—I remember that very well.

She did write in the diary that if she had a choice after the war, she wanted to become a writer in the Netherlands.

As I remember it, she was a bit spoiled, particularly by her father. Anne was her Daddy's girl; Margot was more like her mother. It's a good thing there were only two children. Mrs. Frank was a little religious, and Margot went in that direction too. Margot always said that after the war, if she could choose, she wanted to be a nurse in Israel.

Everything was very idyllic until Hitler occupied the Netherlands.

————

At first not a lot changed. In October 1940, I got a little sister. She became the pet of the Frank family. Every Sunday, Anne and Margot would want to watch my sister being bathed and

17

fed. Then the three of us would take my sister for a walk in the baby carriage. Margot, especially, was crazy about my sister.

But little by little everything changed. We were no longer permitted to ride on the streetcars; Jews couldn't shop in the stores, except between three o'clock and five, and then only in Jewish shops. Gradually, the Germans began to send out summonses for the work camps—especially to young people. We didn't know then that these camps were really something much worse.

After the sixth grade we couldn't continue our studies where we wanted to. All Jewish children had to go to Jewish schools. And, a special school was set up for us, the Jewish Lyceum in the Voormalige Stadstimmertuinen in Amsterdam. It was across from the existing Jewish high school which had always had Jewish students.

At the Jewish Lyceum Anne and I always sat together. We copied each other's work, and I remember that we were once given extra work as a punishment for that. One day, a teacher grabbed Anne by the collar and put her in another class because he wanted to keep us apart. We had been talking too much. I don't know how it happened, but half an hour later there I was sitting next to her in the other class, and then the teachers just let us sit together.

That's how it always was. Anne already wrote very well then. If she had to do extra work because she'd been talking again, she did it very well. Once she wrote an entire poem that the teacher found so funny that he had to laugh and read it out loud. It began, "*Kwek, kwek, kwek, zei juffrouw Snaterbek* (Quack, quack, quack, said Miss Chatterbox)."

At the end of the first year at the Lyceum, there was a big party. Margot was promoted cum laude; she was really a very good student. Anne and I were barely promoted because we weren't so good in math. I remember that we went home together, and after that I didn't see her for a few days.

———

Mr. Frank's factory, Opekta, produced a substance for making jam. My mother always got the old packages as a gift. Soon after school let out, my mother sent me to the Franks' house to get the scale because she wanted to make jam. It was a beautiful day.

I went as usual to the Franks' house and rang and rang and rang, but no one opened the door. I didn't know why no one answered. I rang again, and finally, Mr. Goudsmit, a tenant, opened the door.

"What do you want? What have you come for?" he asked in astonishment.

"I've come to borrow the scale."

"Don't you know that the entire Frank family has gone to Switzerland?"

I didn't know anything about it. "Why?" I asked.

He didn't know either.

This was a bolt out of the blue. Why had they gone to Switzerland? The only connection the Frank family had with Switzerland was that Otto Frank's mother lived there.

But later it appeared that, in fact, the family had always reckoned that it would get worse for Jews. They had been preparing for a whole year to go into hiding. We didn't know anything about this. You can't talk about something like that. Because if anyone talked, then the whole affair would go amiss.

We couldn't go into hiding because my mother was expecting another baby, and my little sister was only two years old. So we never thought of doing anything like that. Mr. Frank visited us often when my father was depressed about the war and the Germans and how it would all turn out and how terrible everything was. And Mr. Frank would always say, "Everything is fine; the war is almost over."

I have often been asked why Mr. Frank chose that other

family, the Van Daans, to join them in hiding and not us, because we were such close friends. But you mustn't forget: in the first place, I had a little two-year-old sister, and with a little girl, you can't go into hiding. In the diary, it tells how they couldn't flush the toilet and could only move a bit freely during the evening. Such measures are naturally impossible with a two-year-old. In the second, my mother was pregnant again, and a woman expecting a baby is also not much good in hiding. For those reasons we never resented it. I never considered it to be a problem.

And so I went home and said to my mother, "No Frank family; here's the scale."

My parents got very upset; they couldn't understand what had happened. But on the way home, I'd met a friend who said, "You know what? I received a letter from the Germans. Next week, I have to go to an *Arbeitslager* (work camp)." He was sixteen years old. Then we put two and two together and figured that perhaps Margot was also supposed to go to that *Lager.* Later, that appeared to have been the case. Margot had been sent a summons, saying that she had to go to such an *Arbeitslager.* It was at that moment that Mr. Frank said, "You aren't going to the *Arbeitslager;* we're going into hiding."

We had no idea that the family had been making preparations for a year. I learned that only after the war, from Mr. Frank. And of course we didn't know that they had actually stayed in Amsterdam. We knew that his mother lived in Switzerland, so we believed that the Frank family had fled to Switzerland. By spreading this rumor, they hoped that there would be no further search for them. At that time, a lot of Jews tried to escape across the border to Switzerland, so that wasn't anything unusual. Most of them were not successful.

———

I believe that Anne was the first girlfriend that I lost. It was, of course, very frightening, but we began to get used to the idea. When I went back to school after the summer, fewer children came to class every day.

We stayed in Amsterdam almost a full year longer, until June 20, 1943, and all this time things were getting worse and worse. Jews had to wear a yellow star. We had an *Ausweis* (an identification card), with a large "J" on it—for Jew. People were stopped on the street: "May I see your *Ausweis?*" If you were Jewish, you were taken away and you never returned home. And a mother waiting for her child would ask herself: Where is my child? Have they taken her away?

It became more dangerous every day. And day by day our classroom became emptier. We arrived in the morning and this boy would no longer be there and that girl wouldn't be there. I shall never forget how Mr. Presser, our history teacher, who later became Professor Presser, gave us a lecture about the Renaissance. He began to read to us about the meeting of Dante and Beatrice in paradise. Suddenly, in the middle of the lesson, he began to cry and ran out of the class.

"What's the matter?"

"Last night they took away my wife."

It was terrible. I still get chills when I think about it, seeing that man standing in front of the class. He had no children, I thought. His wife was everything to him. He went home and his wife wasn't there. That's how it was.

So far, my family had been lucky insofar as we were able to buy South American citizenship through an uncle in Switzerland. We were expatriates. That's why it was possible. We got passports from Paraguay. Laughing, my father said, "You'd better know something about Paraguay in case they ask." So I learned the name of the capital, Asunción. I didn't know anything else, but no one ever asked me anything.

Because of these passports we could still go out for a while longer without trembling in fear, but you never knew what would happen tomorrow.

And then a second document helped us. My father had been,

after all, one of the leaders of the Mizrachi in Germany, and he was also active in the Mizrachi movement in the Netherlands. I believe forty acknowledged lists were drafted and recognized by the Germans, with the names of the most famous Zionists—people who wanted to go to Eretz Israel—and we were on the second list.

So we continued to live, with little to eat and with a great deal of fear, but at least we were at home. In October, my mother died during childbirth. The baby was born dead. That was in Anne's diary. Someone told Anne that our baby had died, but not that my mother had died too. They probably didn't have the heart to tell her.

I can still remember that my father asked whether my sister and I wanted to go into hiding. I refused because our names were on my father's passport and if someone had seen them, my father would have been deported to Auschwitz immediately. I don't know whether I knew then what Auschwitz was, but I knew that if someone was arrested and if all the people who belonged with him weren't there—it would be assumed that they had gone into hiding—he would go to an "S" camp (a punishment camp). So I said to my father, "No, we're going together." We probably still dreamed of staying together.

I do know that our maid was picked up and didn't come back. My father had been able to rescue her once before, but the second time she was taken away. Then there were just the three of us—my father, my little sister, and I. Our grandparents, who had come to the Netherlands from Germany in 1938, lived in the house next door.

Everything went along fine until June 20, 1943, when there was the big roundup in Amsterdam-South. On that day, the Germans started something new. At five o'clock in the morning while everyone was asleep they blocked off all the southern part of Amsterdam. They went from door to door, rang, and asked:

"Do Jews live here?"

"Yes."

22

"You have fifteen minutes; take a backpack, put a few things in it, and get outside quickly."

That was our neighborhood, so we had to pack too. A passport no longer helped. We had a quarter of an hour, and we had to go with them.

Sometimes people ask me: "How could you go with them just like that?" "Why didn't you defend yourself?" Or, "Why didn't you say anything?" That was impossible. There were hundreds of Germans with weapons, and you were alone; you were powerless. And if, once in a while, someone did something, then all of the others would be severely punished. So we couldn't do anything. We were taken away in trucks. A German woman, a neighbor—not Jewish—had only been living under us with her husband for half a year. She was very fond of my sister. She went to the German officer and begged him, "Can't I at least take that little girl?"

And the man shouted back at her, "Aren't you ashamed as a Dutch Christian?"

And she said, "Oh no, I am a German Christian, and I am not ashamed," and she fainted.

So we were taken to Westerbork. My father ended up in a very large barracks. My sister and I were put in an orphanage, where, they said, there was more to eat. My father had known the director of the orphanage when he was in Germany. My little sister wasn't there very long. She became seriously ill and had to have operations on both ears. She was in the hospital for almost the entire time that we were in Westerbork.

I worked there. The toilets were outside, and everyone was very happy when I volunteered to clean them. No one knew why I was so eager to do it. But, now and then, my father was able to come by, and if I was cleaning the toilets just then, I could see him for a moment. That's the reason I did that disgusting work.

It was, in fact, bearable in the orphanage. There were teachers and we still got lessons. There were only youngsters, children of Jews who had been in hiding. The children had been

23

found, but not their parents. It also happened the other way around—that the parents were already gone and the children found later.

Every Friday and Tuesday, trains would come which had to be filled and which then went to Poland. We still had our South American papers and they made it possible for us to stay.

I remember the terrible November night, when it was announced that of all the Palestine lists (lists of people who wanted to go to Israel), only the first two were still valid. All the people on the other lists had to leave that same night. Then the entire orphanage was emptied. I remember Rabbi Vorst, who took all those children and laid a large *tallit* (prayer shawl) over them and blessed them. Most of the teachers went because they wanted to stay with the children. That was awful. On the Friday afternoon after the train left, the only ones still there were me, my sister in the hospital, and two or three other children. All of the rest who had been on those lists disappeared.

On February 15, 1944, neither our Palestine papers nor our passports could help any more. But the big difference for us was that we weren't sent to Auschwitz. If we had been sent to Auschwitz in 1943, I wouldn't be able to tell about it now. Because those people who were taken away in the beginning were almost all killed.

But then I didn't know what Auschwitz was. People talked about an *Arbeitslager* (a work camp) in the east. We were going to an *Austauschlager* (exchange camp). I said at the time: "The Germans want to keep us alive so that they can exchange us for German soldiers."

On February 15, 1944, we were transported to Bergen-Belsen. That was a somewhat better camp. What was better about it? In the first place, we were transported in passenger cars and not in cattle cars. And then, when we arrived, our clothes weren't taken away and families weren't separated. My father and my sister stayed with me. We slept in different

24

places, but we could see each other every evening. The trip took—I don't remember precisely—two or three days to get to Bergen-Belsen.

I don't know any longer whether I knew right away what it meant to be in a concentration camp, but I remember very well how, upon our arrival, the German soldiers stood next to each other, with large dogs at their sides. To this day I am afraid of dogs. I don't believe that experience is the real reason; but if someone remarks about it, then I say, "If you had been there, and if you had seen those dogs, then you'd be afraid, too."

Afterward we had to walk, walk, and walk still farther, until we saw a large field, with barbed wire here and barbed wire there. There were many different camps. But we didn't know who was in there and where they came from. We saw them for the first time later on, when we went to the shower, which was near the train station—a half-hour or an hour walk—but we never had further contact with them.

We came to a part of the camp that was almost new. There were, at most, forty or fifty Jews from Greece there. They became, of course, our bosses, because they had already been there for a while. They distributed the food and had all the important jobs. The doctor was a Greek Jew from Salonika. The camp was called Alballalager.

The first few days, we were separated, but later we were able to be together. In the beginning, my father had to go into a quarantined barracks. Our clothes weren't taken away; that was one of the good things about that camp. In Bergen-Belsen, it was very cold in the winter. We soon found that out. Because we had been arrested in June we hadn't thought about winter clothes. Especially me, a young girl, who had to do her own packing. But what I had brought, I kept.

My sister had a large bandage on her head because she had had surgery on her ears in Westerbork. The first day we arrived in Bergen-Belsen, I got jaundice. The policy of the Germans was: whoever got sick had to go to the hospital; otherwise, all the others could be infected. I didn't know what to do with my little sister. My father was confined in another barracks and I couldn't take her to him. He also had to work, so that wouldn't have worked out.

So there I was and didn't know what to do. This situation showed me that there were very special people in that camp. I told an old lady that I was at my wits' end: "Tomorrow morning, I have to go to the hospital and my little sister is sick."

Two hours later, a woman came, who said, "My name is Abrahams. Mrs. Lange told me that you were here and that you don't know what to do with your sister. I have seven children; give her to me; then we'll just have one more little child with us."

And that's how it worked out. The next morning her daughter, who seemed to be about my age, came and took the little girl with her. Meanwhile, my father was able to visit me. We were together with that family until the end. To this day we have stayed on friendly terms with them.

Every day, we were counted. The Germans were afraid that we would run away, but we couldn't go anywhere. Where could you possibly go, with a large Star of David on your clothes, without money, and without anything? But that was the craziness of the Germans. We had to stand in rows of five for hours in order to be counted.

One day, we looked in the direction where there hadn't been any barracks and saw that tents had suddenly appeared there. It was already quite cold, and we didn't know who was in those tents. Two or three months later, there were very strong wind storms and they were all blown down. On that same day, we received an order: our beds, which were stacked in two levels, one above the other, were taken away, and we got stacks of three beds. Two of us had to sleep in one bed, and half the camp had to be emptied. Then a barbed-wire fence was built through the middle of the camp and filled with straw so that we couldn't see the other side. But we were, of course, very close to each other, because the camp wasn't large. All those people from the tents were taken to the barracks on the other side. In spite of the German guards on the high watchtowers, we tried to make contact. It was, of course, strictly forbidden to talk with those people, and if the Germans saw or heard someone doing that, that person would have been shot at once. Because of that some of us went to the fence after dark to try to pick up something. I never went there, but we learned that they were all people who had come from Poland—Jews and non-Jews.

About a month later, in early February when there was snow on the ground, one of my acquaintances, an older woman, came up to me one day. "Do you know, there are some Dutch people there. I spoke to Mrs. Van Daan." The woman had known her from before, and she told me that Anne was there. She knew that I knew Anne.

"Go over to the barbed-wire fence and try to talk to her." And, of course, I did. In the evening, I stood by the barbed-wire fence and began to call out. And quite by chance Mrs. Van Daan was there again. I asked her, "Could you call Anne?"

She said, "Yes, yes, wait a minute, I'll go to get Anne. I can't get Margot; she is very, very ill and is in bed."

But naturally I was much more interested in Anne, and I waited there a few minutes in the dark.

Anne came to the barbed-wire fence—I couldn't see her. The fence and the straw were between us. There wasn't much light. Maybe I saw her shadow. It wasn't the same Anne. She was a broken girl. I probably was, too, but it was so terrible. She immediately began to cry, and she told me, "I don't have any parents anymore."

I remember that with absolute certainty. That was terribly sad, because she couldn't have known anything else. She thought that her father had been gassed right away. But Mr. Frank looked very young and healthy, and of course the Germans didn't know how old everybody was who they wanted to gas, but selected them on the basis of their appearance. Someone who looked healthy had to work, but another who might even be younger, but who was sick or looked bad, went directly to the gas chamber.

I always think, if Anne had known that her father was still alive, she might have had more strength to survive, because she died very shortly before the end—only a few days before [liberation]. But maybe it was all predestined.

So we stood there, two young girls, and we cried. I told her about my mother. She hadn't known that; she only knew that the baby had died. And I told her about my little sister. I told her that my father was in the hospital. He died two weeks later; he was already very sick. She told me that Margot was seriously ill and she told me about going into hiding because I was, of course, extremely curious.

"But what are you doing here? You were supposed to be in Switzerland, weren't you?" And then she told me what had happened. That they didn't go to Switzerland at all and why they had said that; so that everyone should think that they had gone to her grandmother's.

Then she said, "We don't have anything at all to eat here, almost nothing, and we are cold; we don't have any clothes and I've gotten very thin and they shaved my hair." That was terrible for her. She had always been very proud of her hair. It may have grown back a bit in the meantime, but it certainly wasn't the long hair she'd had before, which she playfully curled around her fingers. It was much worse for them than for us. I said, "They didn't take away our clothes." That was our first meeting.

Then for the first time—we had already been in the camp for more than a year; we arrived in February 1944, and this was February 1945—we received a very small Red Cross package: my sister, my father, and I. A very small package, the size of a book, with *knäckebrot* (Scandinavian crackers), and a few cookies. You can't imagine how little that was. My son always says, "But Mama, that was something really very special." But in those days we really collected everything, half a cookie, a sock, a glove—anything that gave a little warmth or something to eat. My friends also gave me something for Anne. I certainly couldn't have thrown a large package over the barbed-wire fence; not that I had one, but that wouldn't have been possible at all.

We agreed to try to meet the next evening at eight o' clock—I believe I still had a watch. And, in fact, I succeeded in throwing the package over.

But I heard her screaming, and I called out, "What happened?"

And Anne answered, "Oh, the woman standing next to me caught it, and she won't give it back to me."

Then she began to scream.

I calmed her down a bit and said, "I'll try again but I don't know if I'll be able to." We arranged to meet again, two or three days later, and I was actually able to throw over another package. She caught it; that was the main thing.

After these three or four meetings at the barbed-wire fence in Bergen-Belsen, I didn't see her again, because the people in Anne's camp were transferred to another section in Bergen-Belsen. That happened around the end of February.

That was the last time I saw Anne alive and spoke to her.

During that time, my father died, on February 25, 1945, and I didn't go out for a few days. When I went to look for her again, I found that the section was empty.

Then we were supposed to be exchanged. On the evening my father died, one of the doctors came to say who could go and who couldn't. It was quite remarkable, because after all, he saw that my father couldn't go, but still he picked him, possibly because I had pleaded with him, saying that I wouldn't go otherwise. And they dressed him in proper clothes, but the exchange didn't take place after all.

My father died in those clothes. Perhaps he knew or hoped, My daughters may get out. It never happened; only one group was exchanged, and they in fact did arrive in Palestine. Another group was exchanged in the beginning of 1945, but they stayed in Biberach until the liberation.

29

At the end of March, my grandmother died, and in the beginning of April we had to completely evacuate the camp. Only those who were dangerously ill could stay behind. I had typhus. I was indeed sick, but not mortally ill, so I had to go. I still remember that we had to spend an entire night in the open air waiting for the trains to come, and then a very long train came. There was one passenger car; the Germans were in that car—twenty escort troops, and there were—I don't know anymore how many—forty or fifty cattle cars, and we were put into them, we—that was the people from our camp and also some from the camp with Hungarian Jews next to ours.

This train was headed for one or another gas chamber, probably Theresienstadt. We never arrived there. Germany was in the last phase of a terrible war and the train couldn't go any farther. There was gun fire from all sides, and we had to get out of the train and lie in the fields. The train couldn't get through anywhere and certainly not to its destination.

There was nothing to eat. I still remember that a German soldier gave my sister a cookie one day. I thought, That is God himself.

There was also a train with German soldiers, and I had a ring from my grandmother and one from my mother and four other families gave their rings. For all those rings, six or eight of them, we got a little rabbit from those German soldiers. We didn't have anything to eat, you see. And if we had died, we wouldn't have needed those rings anyway. A woman cooked that rabbit on a wood fire, and so we had something to eat.

Otherwise, there was no food on that train. Then the Germans said, "Whoever is strong enough can go to German farmers in the neighborhood to ask for something to eat." An old woman took care of my sister, so I could go, taking turns with her son.

It was very risky to go to those villages for food because you never knew when the train would leave. The brother of one of my girlfriends missed the train. He went to look for food and when he came back, the train was gone. He was rescued, really through a miracle. But I couldn't afford to do that; I was alone with my sister whom I had to take care of, so I always had little to eat because I could only look for food near the train.

That went on for about ten days, when we woke up one morning and saw the Germans with white flags in their hands. We couldn't get over it. What had happened? The Russians had come, and the first thing they did was to seize the Germans. They didn't know exactly what to do with us, and it was probably a terrible sight—all those Jews and sick people, thin as rails.

There were two villages in the area, Trobitz and Schilda (near Frankfurt an der Oder), maybe more, but I remember those two. The village of Trobitz had not surrendered and was still fighting the Russians. That was our good fortune. The Russians said, "Go ahead, you are going to get those Germans out of their houses; then you can live in those houses." Now I was just a young girl with an even smaller sister; I couldn't get any Germans out of their houses, and when I got there, everything was already full. I was still with that older woman and her son and one or two other families.

Then someone pointed out that there was another village where the inhabitants had raised white flags. So you wouldn't have to push anyone out of their house; you only had to look for an empty one. We found one—it was a little less than a mile farther on, and I still remember that we got the mayor's house. The first night of freedom, I slept in his daughter's bed; she had left a dress hanging there that fit me. The ceiling was light green, with dark green swastikas. So the first night of freedom, I slept with swastikas over my head, but I turned my back to them.

The people in that village had a great deal to eat—they were farmers. The mayor wasn't a farmer and didn't have much in

31

his cellar, so we went to ask the Russians, although we were a little afraid. They gave us "ration cards", which I still have, to get milk, bread, and sausage from a store.

We always tried to keep in touch with the other village (Trobitz). In the meantime, the Russians had given lists with our names to the Americans. I don't know exactly anymore—I think that it was on June 15—the Americans got permission to take us away in trucks. They took us out of the Russian zone and brought us to Leipzig. We stayed there two or three days in a school, and after that we rode for four days in a wonderful American train back to the Dutch border. There we got something to eat, but we had to be very careful not to eat too much—we were all much too weak. That is the only time in my life that I ever ate pork, out of a can.

At the border, we went to a beautiful, large castle—I've forgotten the name—but the castle was full of people. We asked, "Who are they?" And it turned out they were NSB (members of the Dutch Nazi organization which had collaborated with the Germans) whom the Dutch wanted to send to Germany. So they had to receive us there when we arrived from Germany. That was, of course, not very pleasant, but we didn't speak to them, and a day later they were taken away.

In Maastricht, everyone was examined and they found something in my lungs. So I couldn't go farther. I had to go into the hospital in Maastricht immediately. There, there were very friendly Catholic nuns and an awfully nice Indian doctor. I stayed there from about July first to September.

But I had a big surprise in Maastricht. One day, they told me that I had a visitor. So I dressed myself very nicely, with things I had been given by Dutch people; we had been adopted by a couple of Christian families. They gave us clothes and brought us treats—very good people. And who stood there, suddenly before me? Mr. Frank! And I was so happy. I couldn't wait to tell him: "Your daughter is alive." And I told him that, and he answered, "No." He had already learned that she was no longer living, but I didn't know that because when I had last seen her, she was still alive.

He had seen our names—my sister's and mine—on a list. My sister was already in a children's home in Laren and he had looked her up there. He told me everything that had happened to him.

We began to think about what we ought to do. Mr. Frank's mother lived in Switzerland, and he knew my uncle there. He had made contact—it didn't work the way it does now. The postal service wasn't working yet; Mr. Frank had to travel six or eight hours to Maastricht from Amsterdam.

He became my father from then on; he took care of everything. In September, I arrived in Amsterdam, and Mr. Frank arranged for papers to go to Switzerland. I know the exact date: December fifth. I wear a necklace with a pendant: the queen is on one side and Mr. Frank had them engrave "December 5, 1945" on the other side. That was the day that he took me, my sister, and a girlfriend and her sister to Switzerland. He himself took us on the plane. My uncle came from Geneva to Zurich to pick us up, and Mr. Frank went to visit his mother.

In Switzerland, I at first entered a sanitarium, but my dream was to go to Palestine; all my upbringing was directed toward that. No one dreamed then of a Jewish state. Or rather, everyone dreamed about it, but we didn't believe it was possible. All my efforts were devoted to: How can I get there as quickly as possible?

But it wasn't possible simply to travel to Palestine at that time because the English allowed so few Jews to get in. My uncle didn't approve of my going illegally. He said, "You've been through enough. Wait until we get a certificate (that's what it was called) for you."

Until it arrived, I went to school in Switzerland, for about a year, and I saw Mr. Frank again there. I visited his mother often. I lived in Basel, and she did too. Whenever he came, I went to visit him.

33

Before I went to Israel, I wanted to return to Amsterdam once more, healthy and well, to see everything—the school and where we had lived and, of course, Mr. Frank. He went with me to see a friend from our class who was still very sick. Later, in Israel, I naturally also kept in touch with him—always. He was Uncle Otto. We continued to write to each other for every birthday and every New Year's.

In 1963, he came to Israel for the first time and saw my children. I still remember that we, the whole family, wanted to go to his hotel. But he said, "Oh no, I want to see your children, don't I? Children have to be seen in their own surroundings." That was so nice, and then he came and picked the children up and played with them. The children were crazy about him because of his extraordinary personality.

We always kept in touch with Otto Frank, and with his second wife, Fritzi. He really became happy again. I have asked myself: How can you live like that, only in the past? Apparently he was able to set that aside. I don't believe that he was a broken man later.

JANNY BRANDES-BRILLESLIJPER

Janny Brandes-Brilleslijper.

Full of doubts, I began my first visit to Janny Brandes in her house on the Amstel river near the Carré Theater in Amsterdam. The place, however, gave me courage. Born and brought up on the Amstel myself, less than 200 meters from Janny's house, I felt that I was in familiar surroundings. It would take considerable effort and persuasion to convince Janny to tell her story. The Director of the Royal Institute for War Documentation, who had only spoken with her on the telephone, predicted a difficult road ahead. He was right. Many conversations followed that first awkward visit and eventually led to a relationship of trust and friendship. A year and a half later, we filmed the interview in one day.

Janny's relationship with Anne and the Frank family began on August 8, 1944. They met at Central Station in Amsterdam, the starting point for the deportations to the Westerbork camp. Janny had been arrested because she worked in the resistance against the Nazis. She was born into a Jewish-socialist environment in the heart of the old Jewish quarter in Amsterdam, but married a man who was not Jewish. From the very beginning, both of them fought as anti-Fascists against the Nazis. In the summer of 1944, she was arrested in her own house with her family and several others who were in hiding there. Her husband, Bob, and her two children were able to escape.

Janny kept in touch with Anne and Margot in Bergen-Belsen right up to the end in March 1945. She used her strong personality and her ability to get things done to nurse sick people—if one can even speak of nursing under such wretched circumstances—thanks to a course in first aid she had once taken.

Janny survived Auschwitz-Birkenau and Bergen-Belsen together with her sister, Lientje Rebling-Brilleslijper, who sang under the name Lin Jaldati and who died recently in East Germany. In 1946, Janny wrote to Otto Frank to notify him of the deaths of his daughters Margot and Anne.

Janny Brandes-Brilleslijper

I was born in 1916 on Nieuwe Kerkstraat in Amsterdam, close to the Weesperstraat. My parents had a store in which they sold groceries and delicacies. I had an older sister and a younger brother. My father and mother both worked very hard in the store. When my mother was in the store, my sister or a helper had to look after the children, which is not to say that we were neglected; there were very strong bonds in our family. My parents used every minute of free time they had to include us in their concerns.

We really never had any contact with the authorities, and the neighborhood had something to do with that. We lived in the old Jewish quarter, but we weren't religious. We never went to the shul. Father was a socialist in his fashion. He sang in the *Stem des Volks* (a socialist singing group). He had a marvelous voice and from the time that we were young, he sang all the opera arias that he knew for us. When he was shaving, his voice rang through the entire house. We lived over the store.

On Friday evenings, my parents closed the shop early, and

then the large lamp above the table would be turned on and the table set. This was not for religious reasons; it was a tradition. When as little girls we'd visit people, and they asked us if we'd like to stay to eat, I always asked, "Is it Friday?" Because on Fridays, we always went home. And later, when we were bigger and more independent, we'd go home on Friday evenings and bring our friends so that they could enjoy the Friday evening atmosphere.

My father was a wonderful storyteller, and on Friday evenings he would always talk about something from the Torah. It was not that he wanted to be religious, but he thought that this should be part of our upbringing. He started with Adam and Eve and told about all sorts of crazy, *meshuge,* experiences that Adam and Eve had in Paradise. I've often told my children how Eve let Adam take a bite of the apple and then suddenly the thundering voice of God said, "Adam, what are you doing?" and then Adam said, "Oh, God, I'm here, but I don't dare to come out, because I'm completely naked"—and so began the Fall of Man.

That's how we learned how it all fit together. We were believers, but we were not religious. In the background, there was indeed our own God, for God wasn't present, and yet He was. When my mother was particularly worried about something, she would cry, "O God, O God, Mother help me, please." How characteristic of her!

We grew up in this warm and attentive atmosphere despite all the pressures of having both parents working. And we learned how to think independently even when we were still quite young.

We were members of a gymnastics club; my sister had a little friend, who was a member of Hatza'ir, a Zionist organization, and she took me there. I became a member of Hatza'ir as well. There we first became aware of justice and injustice, because we hadn't actually ever encountered discrimination or the sickness in the world. Racism—You don't notice that until you're older.

For instance, when we no longer lived on Kerkstraat, but on Marnixstraat, Father worked at the vegetable market in my grandfather's wholesale grocery business. In Hatza'ir there were children whose parents were intellectuals and people in a higher position, among whom we really didn't belong, since we were children of tradespeople. We went to the best schools that our parents could find, but there was still a class difference that kept us removed. In Hatza'ir we were with the sons and daughters of lawyers and doctors, who were better off. And they stared at us because we were the daughters of a shopkeeper. I didn't take this so much to heart. In fact I protested very indignantly because it was the first time—as a thirteen or fourteen year old—that I was confronted by such haughtiness.

I had already discovered the fact that I was Jewish because we lived then in the Marnixstraat, an overtly non-Jewish neighborhood where the market was and where we went to school. I went to school on Prinsengracht, at the Elisabeth Wolff School. Much later, my granddaughter went to the preparatory school there, which pleases me very much.

My parents paid a lot of attention to our pronunciation of Dutch. My cousins, who lived in the Jewish section, spoke more pronouncedly "Amsterdam" Yiddish than we did. We were teased at family get-togethers. We often visited my grandfather, who lived next to the Jewish orphanage on the Rapenburgerstraat. When we looked out of Grandpa's window, we would see the little orphan boys in the inner courtyard. Sometimes they'd climb up the fire ladders and then they would be scolded. That happened quite frequently.

We were urged to do other things. In their own way, my parents were progressive. My father, after all, was a socialist. My parents had a terrible quarrel with my mother's parents, who thought that my father wasn't refined enough. So, on the first of May, my parents ran away together and were married at the district court, just to show what they thought about that.

They carefully planned their children. The New Malthusian League didn't exist yet, but after it was established, Father became a member, as evidence of his progressiveness. We were all born four years apart. My sister is four years older, my brother is four years younger, precision planning.

At that time, according to the conventional wisdom, girls didn't have to study; they had to learn a trade. Boys could go to high school. Girls got married, so it was a waste to spend a lot of money on them. They did have to know about a lot of things, though.

After elementary school, I went to a high school for a short time, but because I was a little wild and restless, and because my father got into arguments with my teachers, I wasn't allowed to continue there. Probably also because I was "that Jewish kid," Father stood up for me and quarreled with one of the teachers, who turned around and said, "I'll see about you."

My father said to me, "If you don't want to study then go and earn your keep. I don't know how you're going to do it.; I'll help you to get started, but after that, you'll have to figure it out for yourself." I don't think that my father was unreasonable. I was terribly defiant and I was very angry with him. My sister, Lientje, took my side, because we always stood together, but I do believe that, ultimately, he was in the right.

Actually I didn't learn a trade. As a fourteen year old, I was placed in a sewing workshop, but, because I had so little patience, that didn't last long. I lasted only six months there.

A lot of rambling; I did a little of everything. I worked several years in a medical-cosmetics laboratory, which I found very interesting. As we earned money, we could take courses. I took a first-aid course—we'll return to that later—and I learned English, French, and a little German because we often had German servants, so that came easily.

As time went by, we drifted away from Zionism, in which social status counted for a lot. My sister had a friend whose parents were such respectable people. The boy was attending high school and was planning to study medicine. His mother made it very clear to my sister that she would not be the right partner for her son, who would soon become a doctor.

41

While I worked at the laboratory, I went from being a Zionist to becoming a Communist. Although the word, "Communist" isn't the right word. I didn't actually become a member of the party until the beginning of the war; and left it shortly after the war. "Marxist" is a better word, because Marx's idea, that all people should work according to their abilities and receive according to their needs, is actually a good solution; I still think so.

During that time, I met Bob, who had lived for a month in the same building as my sister, who was a dancer at the National Revue. He came from the Hague and worked as an apprentice. He had a room in the house that Lientje had rented from an actress when she appeared for a month on stage with the National Revue at the Stadsschouwburg theater. I was taking folk-dancing lessons then; I had left the Zionist movement. I felt that we had to assimilate and that we belonged with the workers, not with the well-to-do upper crust; that we had to fight for a better society. Bob was a member of the board of the SDSC, the Social Democratic Student Association. We debated with each other constantly; I never agreed with him.

Our marriage was a strange state of affairs; the in-laws did not want their oldest son, who was still a student, to marry a Jewish girl; but in the end they reconciled themselves to it. We had to get married. We had started living together in the Hague in January 1938, and in 1939 we were married. Two months after the wedding, Rob was born. My parents had the shock of their lives. They were really displeased—they would have preferred to have things turn out otherwise.

In 1939, we came face to face with Hitler's Germany. The first year we were married and living on our own, we had already taken in *onderduikers* (people who went into hiding). Alexander de Leeuw, the director of Pegasus, the Communist publishing house, hid with us that winter. Things were already very tense from then until the tenth of May (in 1940).

We had been convinced for a couple of years that war would break out. We figured that out from the reports all around us.

We always hoped that it wouldn't happen. May 10 was a magnificent day, with glorious weather. The sun rose early, (the sky) was a radiant blue, and we heard an uproar, a racket, a noise, that we couldn't describe. We turned on the radio, and then we knew that the war had begun. We were dreadfully frightened.

We had absolutely no experience with the underground, but a great deal had to be done immediately. In the beginning, we thought that the English would support us, and kick the *Moffen* (Dutch expletive for the Nazis) out, but after a day or two, we knew that wouldn't happen. We lived near the royal palace, and we saw the royal family leave in their cars. We understood then that the country would be occupied.

We completely understood what the consequences would be. The fact is, we had already helped a large number of refugees, with the assistance of the International Red Cross. We had tried to get as many people out of Germany as possible. We knew the danger that threatened us. Of this, there was no doubt, as was soon confirmed.

We didn't try to escape. In the middle of the war, we still had the opportunity to go to Switzerland, but you don't desert your home. If there's fighting to be done, you just have to stand and fight. That has always been true. It was that way throughout the war. You have to be true to yourself—you can never be something you are not, and you can't fool yourself. We believed that. We did what we had to do; what we could do. No more and no less.

In the meantime, Bob had found government work, first with the petroleum bureau and later with the central food supply office, and so we were able to stay on our feet. But he did have to interrupt his studies.

From the beginning we were involved with resistance activities. There was no question of our going into hiding. In the first place, Bob wasn't Jewish, and in the second place, we had a child. Actually, I never did go into hiding. That's what was so crazy about the situation. When Bob received questionnaires at his office asking him to report if he, or anyone in his family was Jewish, we read them together, and I can still see his expression of disgust as he picked them up by the corner, opened the cover of our potbellied stove, and let them slowly fall into the fire. "What are you going to do now?" I asked. And he said, "I'm not going to fill out anything, and neither are you. I don't want to have anything to do with this, and whatever happens to us, well, we'll see." So in our indignation, without even realizing it, we handled it in the right way, because I never did turn in my own identity card. And until the day we were arrested I used it in my everyday life. Isn't that remarkable? Actually, we should have told a lot of people that, that above all, they shouldn't do anything. Because I believed it was a cardinal error for people to feel compelled to report themselves for fear that otherwise someone else might.

The first person who came to hide with us was Alex de Leeuw; he was arrested shortly thereafter. The Communist party went underground after the uproar of May 10 and the arrest and subsequent release of Communists. We had already heard about how things went from our German comrades. But of course we made enormous mistakes, because we didn't know just whom we were up against. An awful lot of victims suffered because of our clumsiness, our ignorance, and our underestimation of this evil.

Because Fascism was the evil. And it still exists! It is the worst evil in the world. Setting people against each other because of their skin color or because someone has a little more than someone else.

We opposed it from the start. We lived above a printer, Van Buchheim and Woerlee, where an NSB (Dutch Nazi) leaflet was printed. We had a large upstairs apartment where we could hide quite a number of people. And that's what we did. In the first year of the war, about three months after it started, we mimeographed a leaflet on a hand-run machine which made your hands black; you had to fit the stencil in precisely.

That leaflet was called "Signal," and we distributed it in the

Hague. We got quite a bit of reaction. We didn't give an address, of course; that would have been too dangerous. But every one of us pitched in to help.

Shortly thereafter, we rented a building in the Schilderswijk (the artists' quarter), in order to set up a print shop, because we needed more room.

Our contacts with Amsterdam almost fell apart with the February strike (a public protest against the anti-Jewish Nazi regulations), when an appalling number of people were seized; one by one, all of our go-betweens, our intermediaries were arrested. We were a little afraid of the people who replaced them, because you could never be certain. You would wonder, can he be trusted? But we simply had to trust the passwords, otherwise, we might just as well have given up then and there.

Thus we lived in the middle of the underground. My younger brother, who was then in high school, could no longer go to school. He started a bicycle parking business with a friend. Mail and packages for various people working in the resistance were inconspicuously delivered and picked up there.

August 17, 1941, that is, after the February strike, they came to search our house. Pamphlets with which we had been involved had been distributed in the Hague, although at that time all contacts had fallen off a bit. I was expecting our second child soon. They turned the entire house upside-down. What they were looking for had been stashed in the kitchen, in pots on the top shelf. It was a really stupid place. It was terribly hot that day, and they kept going to the kitchen to drink water. It gave me a fit every time.

The search of the house was conducted by the SD, and Dutch officers as well. Very creepy. They ransacked our bookcases and they took very silly books with them. I had a copy of *Little Johannes,* by Frederik van Eeden, in my bookcase. It had been bound in red leather by a friend of mine who was a bookbinder, and I think they took it because it was red. They tore the bed apart to see if we had anything in there. But everything they were looking for was in the pots and pans up on the kitchen shelf, and fortunately they didn't look there. It turned out all right. That entire evening, I kept a fire going in the stove in order to burn up all those valuable papers.

Our daughter was born three weeks later. It was a difficult time. Bob went into hiding on the day that the house was searched. I didn't have any reason to go into hiding. I was simply a mother with two small children. Shortly thereafter, I had my younger brother, my father, and my mother in the house. It was quite natural for me to do. It happened like this:

In the winter of 1941–42, we had all gone to Amsterdam to visit my parents. Things were going pretty well then. But in the spring of 1942, my brother had to leave. He was warned by the police on the Jonas Daniël Meyerplein that the Nazis were looking for him. So he simply got on the train and went to his sister in the Hague, without giving it any further thought. We really were rather naive. After that they took Father as a hostage. He was half blind and had had two serious eye operations. To us, he was a very old man. He wasn't really because he was fifty, or just past fifty, and I realize that now, now that I'm over seventy. We got Father out, with the help of Benno Stokvis, a half-Jewish lawyer, who knew how to deal with the Nazis.

When my Father was released, Stokvis said that I should take my parents into hiding because the Nazis would certainly come back. We simpletons took them to the Hague—unbelievable, really. They were with their daughter! Right afterward, there were those big raids. My parents were really always lucky in those things, Their neighborhood, the Nieuwe Achtergracht, where there were quite a few people with a bit more money, was ravaged by the Nazis.

So we were all together in the Hague. I continued to do resistance work, to remove the "J's" from "p.b.'s." A "p.b." is an identity card. We scratched out the "J's" with a very sharp knife. People would ring the door bell and ask, "Does Brandes live here?"

"Yes?"

"Could you remove the "J" from my identity card?"

The situation was so dangerous that my father said one morning, "If you don't stop this immediately, I'm going to turn myself in."

So we had to find a way out. My brother-in-law, Jan, whose family lived in Bergen, arranged for a house there. I got official approval to move to Bergen. Lientje and her husband, Eberhard, moved with me. He was a German citizen. At first, he succeeded in being rejected for military service by going on a special starvation diet prescribed for him by a friend who was a doctor. But later, at the next call-up, he went into hiding.

So we got the summer house in Bergen. And Eberhard and Lientje were just a short distance from us in another summer house, also obtained through Jan.

Then, in 1943, Bergen was evacuated. We were at our wits' end. What should we do now? In the meantime, we stayed together. I had about seven people in the house. Lientje and Eberhard also had two people with them in their summer house. In addition to Jews, others were being seized—people who had gone into hiding or people who were to be sent to Germany. There was a lot of shooting in Bergen, because there was a Nazi camp there—a military base and a small military airport.

We had officially moved to Bergen, but how could we get farther? All the areas where we would have wanted to go were blocked off. Then my brother-in-law Jan, through connections, came up with a house in Huizen. It belonged to two young girls, students who were still under-aged. Jan himself was still studying then. We got permission to move to Huizen. So once again we moved legally.

In the meantime, Bob came out of hiding in Bergen and joined us. Through intermediaries, he got back his job with the

Food Commission and was assigned to Laren or Blaricum. That's how we got permission to go to live in Huizen. It was all very official. Eberhard and Lientje, in the meantime, had become Mr. and Mrs. Bosch with a child who was a little asthmatic, and they were able to come with us. They lived half legally with us. The other *onderduikers* who had been living with us—we simply took them along.

The house was called the High Nest, and it was on the Driftweg. A very large house, on a large plot of land and some woods; the land went nearly down to the water. There we had just about every kind of adventure with our *onderduikers* that one could possibly have had.

The work simply went on. Bob was in the Food Supply Commission and managed to steal food for the underground because everybody had to eat. I also worked as a courier; I traveled back and forth between Utrecht, Amsterdam, and the Hague, usually taking a child with me.

One day, in the summer of 1944, I had to be in Amsterdam at the registration office, where we had people who had authentic identity cards ask for the cards of people who had already died, but who had not yet been registered as dead by the registrar. This was a very safe way to help people get good identity cards. People who were seized often said that their card had been forged—which wasn't true—in order to protect the others.

I returned to Huizen with my little boy and with two bags of material. I was very nervous because my appointment in Amsterdam hadn't worked out. We had agreed to meet on the Roelof Hartplein. I can still see myself waiting there, with a child of four or five who was getting terribly impatient.

On the way back, I picked up wheat in Weesp, for dinner. At home, we had an agreed-upon signal. There was a large Chinese vase that stood in front of the window in one of the upstairs rooms. The agreement was that the vase would be removed if there was danger, so that whoever came home would know that it wasn't safe. That day, I wasn't the only one

Anne Frank, age thirteen, in the Jewish Lyceum, Amsterdam, 1942.

Hannah (Hanneli) Pick-Goslar—"Lies Goosens" in Anne's diary—on the Merwedeplein in 1987.

Amsterdam, 1934. In the folding chair, Margot Frank; in the middle, Anne; and Hanneli on the right.

Hanneli with her father, Hans Goslar, on the Merwedeplein in Amsterdam, about 1935.

Hanneli with her little sister in 1941.

In the sandbox of a neighbor's daughter on the Merwedeplein in Amsterdam in 1937. On the left, Hanneli; next to her, Anne.

Anne and Hanneli on the Merwedeplein, May 1939.

Verjaardagspardijdje van
Anne Frank. 12-6-1939

l. naar rechts:
Lucie v. Dijk
Anne Frank
Suzanne Ledermann
Hannili Goslar
Juultje Ketellaper

16

Anne at the Montessori School.

OPPOSITE: *Anne with her friends. From left to right: Lucie van Dijk, Anne Frank, Suzanne Ledermann, Hanneli Goslar, Juultje Ketellapper, Kitty Egyedi, Mary Bos, Rie (Ietje) Swillens, and Martha van den Berg.*
INSET: *"Anne Frank's birthday party, 12-6-39." Anne wrote this to Hanneli Goslar on the back of the picture taken on Anne's tenth birthday.*

The Frederik School on the Voormalige Stadstimmertuinen in Amsterdam was used during the war as a Jewish Lyceum. A German regulation required Jewish students to attend this school. Anne and Hannah were here together for several years. On the opposite side of the street is the Jewish high school, which is still in operation.

The kindergarten class of the Sixth Public Montessori School in Amsterdam-South in 1935, where Anne (circled at the right) and Hanneli (circled at the left) spent seven years together. On the basis of this classic photograph, Jan Wiegal, who was himself in this class, made the film **The Class** *in 1969.*

Hannah Pick-Goslar, during the filming of the television documentary, in front of the Sixth Public Montessori School in Amsterdam-South, which is now named after Anne Frank. Words from Anne's diary are on the façade.

Janny Brandes-Brilleslijper in the spring of 1941 in Amsterdam.

In 1939, Janny Brilleslijper married Bob Brandes.

Janny and Bob with their children, Rob and Lilo, shortly after the liberation.

Rachel van Amerongen–Frankfoorder at the beginning of the war.

*Bloeme Emden at the Jewish Lyceum,
December 17, 1941.*

*Photograph of the fourth class in the Jewish Lyceum in Amsterdam, taken in the school year, 1941–42.
Bloeme Emden sits in front, just to the right of the center.*

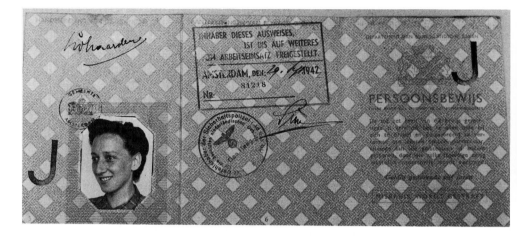

Lenie de Jong–van Naarden's identification card, issued by the Sicherheitspolizei *in 1941, with the letter "J" prominently shown.*

Ronnie van Cleef in September 1940.

Hannah Pick-Goslar, back in her classroom, after forty-seven years. The interior is nearly in its original state.

doing underground work, several couriers visited us. None of them knew about the others.

I don't know who betrayed us. They were all inside when I arrived with my wheat. I had indeed noticed that the vase was gone, but my little daughter was still inside. I can't imagine that anyone could run away under those circumstances.

My son Rob ran to the front door; I had sent him ahead to ask if someone could help me carry the bags because they were extremely heavy. I put the bags behind the bushes and went on. I rang the bell—a strange sensation, to ring the bell at your own house. The door was opened. A man stood at the door and said, "Who are you?"

I replied immediately, "May I ask who you are?"

He pulled me inside by the arm and slapped my face. Rob stood next to me and screamed, "Mama!" Naturally that upset me.

It was a terrible situation. We had *onderduikers* in every room in the house. My younger brother had made a hiding place in every room to escape to if there was danger. We also had an alarm signal. Under the carpet on the stairs, there was a bell which you could press with your foot and this would set off an alarm that would ring in each room. Then one knew that something was wrong. The bell had indeed been used and most of them had gotten to their hiding places. They'd caught me already, and Lientje and Eberhard, who were also downstairs. We tried to communicate with our eyes. But there was nowhere to turn.

My little daughter was sick; she had a fever, and we had called the doctor. He was allowed to take the children—all three. That is Katinka, Lientje's child, went too. The doctor hesitated between saying yes or no because he was only partially aware of the underground work in our house. But in the end, the children were allowed to go with him. Later that caused quite some difficulty, because when my parents-in-law came to pick up the children, they had to abduct Katinka, since the Nazis had found out that she was the daughter of an unmarried Jewish woman. The Nazis even tried to get the child back, but thank God they didn't succeed.

We knew that the police in Huizen were good people and that they had warned Bob at his office not to go home till later. Then, the doctor called him to tell him that he had the children. Bob took them to his parents.

The Nazis had to search for days before they had all of the people who had gone into the hiding places, because it wasn't so easy to find them. Some of them were in there for three days. They were starving, for although there was a small amount of food in the secret hiding places, there wasn't enough for three days. And they also had to relieve themselves.

In the end, everyone was seized. We were first brought to the Naarden fortress, and later, one by one, we were, brought, via the Marnixstraat, to the Euterpestraat in Amsterdam. When Loes and Bram Texeira de Mattos and their children (*onderduikers* who lived with us) and I arrived, Lientje and Eberhard were already there. Father and Mother arrived later. We were interrogated for days on end: Eberhard, a German, and Janny Brandes-Brilleslijper, a Jewish woman. They couldn't understand the connection between her and that German.

By then, Lientje had already left. They interrogated Eberhard and me and tried to play us off against each other. They didn't succeed. At police headquarters they allowed us to be together in the evenings, and this was our salvation. Then we would know how far we could go the next day. We tried to say as little as possible.

I was interrogated right up to the moment that Eberhard escaped. After that, they simply beat me in a blind rage, but I was no longer interrogated. Had they kept it up, I might have said things that I didn't want to tell. None of us gave anyone away. I don't know whether you should pride yourself on that or not. We didn't put anyone in danger.

The last time that we were being taken from our house on Marnixstraat—we had to go to the Spaarndammerdijk—Eberhard jumped off the prison van. I held onto the guard just long enough for Eberhard to get as far up the street as possible. Then the guy pushed me away and began to shout, but Eberhard had already disappeared. I was brought into the Spaarndam police bureau.

I had fainted, and the police guarded me until the Nazis came back and we drove back to Euterpestraat. They began to let out their anger on me in the elevator. I was beaten and thrown against the bars of the elevator. They slapped me around. They were Germans; Willy Lages, the head of the German SD in Amsterdam, stood on my legs with his boots. They really battered and bruised my legs, but they didn't interrogate me again.

After they had beaten me, I was shut up in a cellar on Euterpestraat for twenty-four hours—for me, an eternity. When they came to take me out, I thought, Now, I'll be shot; oh well. . . . In my thoughts, I had said goodbye to everything. And then, to my amazement, I went to the prison for convicts on the Amstelveenseweg.

There it seemed that they didn't actually know anything about me. I was simply put in a cell, where I stayed for about six weeks. There were six people—sometimes even eight—in a cell meant for two. There was a woman, Tante Betje, from the Jordaan (a working-class neighborhood in Amsterdam), who had been arrested. She couldn't understand why she had been picked up, because she only had two Jewish grandfathers. Can you imagine that?

In the mornings, we would get a small cup of water to wash with and then Tante Betje would cry out, "Girls, wash your cunts!" We laughed so much, you know. It wasn't all tears. . . . We tried to keep each other going.

At the beginning of August, we were taken out of the cells early one morning. It was a very quiet summer morning, beautiful weather, the sun was shining, there was morning dew, and the cold of the night still hung over the city. Under guard we left the Amstelveenseweg and took the streetcar to the

Central Station, entering by a side entrance, and then walking on the little paving stones to the platform.

At the same time, another group of people arrived, among them Anne Frank and the Frank family. It struck me that the two girls were dressed in sporty clothes, with sweatsuits and backpacks, as if they were going on a winter vacation. The situation was somewhat unreal—the quiet of that morning and all those people being brought to the train.

The train had compartments closed off by doors on both sides. You stepped inside and then you sat there. I observed the girls attentively, but we didn't speak with each other during the trip.

When we arrived in Westerbork, we were terribly upset, for after all we didn't know where we were going. We saw each other again on the platform. That day, we were all interned in the "S" barracks (the punishment barracks)—the Frank family, too. We all had our own problems, of course. I found my sister again there, and my parents and my brother, and we didn't pay very much attention to what was going on around us. But still, a family like that, with two children. We knew that they were there, that they had been in hiding. What a shame to have been caught at the last minute.

Once in a while, we talked with each other. For example, when we were breaking up batteries. . . . That was very messy work, and no one could understand the reason for it. We had to chop open the batteries with a chisel and a hammer and then throw the tar in one basket and the carbon bars, which we had to remove, into another basket; we had to take off the metal caps with a screwdriver, and they went into a third basket. In addition to getting terribly dirty from the work, we all began to cough because it gave off a certain kind of dust. The agreeable part of working on the batteries was that you could talk with each other. It was such dreary work that you could exchange your thoughts.

I know that my sister Lientje, especially, had contact with the mother of the girls, Edith Frank. The Frank girls were there, too. We sat at long tables while we split the batteries. There was talk, there was laughter. You kept your sorrow to yourself because you never talked about things of a more serious nature. You could never know whether you might not be endangering another person.

We thought by now there wouldn't be another transport. Through the IPA, the Israelite Press Agency—that's what we called rumors, the nonsense plucked from the air, but the IPA sustained us—we heard about the approach of the Russians and the advances of the Americans and that the English had almost reached Arnhem. That last was true, but we didn't know that.

Suddenly, came the alarming news that there would be another transport, and we were all terribly frightened. Everyone tried to avoid the transport. One invented all kinds of terrible, strange illnesses because in Westerbork there were the best surgeons and doctors who were prepared to do a great deal for people. But since we were in the "S" barracks, we had scarcely any contact with them, only by roundabout ways. One of the IPA stories that we heard promised that liberation was at hand and that it would be only a little longer before we would be liberated. Then we went on the transport. So the despair was so much the greater, because there'd be little chance that we'd be alive for the liberation.

We knew that Auschwitz was a death camp. So we knew what to expect. We did our utmost to avoid it. We were political prisoners and we tried to disguise our Jewishness. Benno Stokvis had gotten my father out of jail on the pretext that my mother, who was named Gerritse, wasn't Jewish. In the same way, we tried to be counted as political prisoners so that we wouldn't be put into a Jewish work camp. We knew that the Jewish work camp meant the end. The absolute end. We knew that. Although it was scanty, there was information about those camps. Then while we were being transported, we only hoped that we weren't going to Auschwitz, Treblinka, or Majdanek—camps that were already notorious.

When we were called up for the transport, a sort of panic broke out. Everyone tried to hide behind someone else, or through connections to get an exemption or at least a postponement. Every day that you could stay free might protect you and allow you to remain in the Netherlands to experience the liberation. At that time, everyone was running around. I know that Otto Frank went all over the place. He had the illusion that he could go to Theresienstadt. There were a lot of people who thought that they would be safer in Theresienstadt, with more protection. That turned out to be a pipe dream.

So before the last transport, everyone did their best to save themselves. We just tried to stay together. We knew that some people we had gotten to know were going to try to jump off the train, so we tried to get into the cars with them, so that we, too, could hazard that chance. But when the names were called, everything went amiss. We embraced our parents for the last time. My brother went with my parents.

My sister Lientje and I were kept together since we were political prisoners. So we didn't end up in the same cattle car as my parents. We made no effort to join them, since if someone escaped, the whole family would be punished. That was part of the procedure.

We imagined that we and our parents were as safe as possible. If the war were to last only a short time longer, we thought they would make it, because they weren't so old. In Auschwitz, we saw them once, from a distance, on the station platform.

During the trip, we stood—or tried to sit. Some people had brought stools with them. Everyone had brought things in a bag or a backpack. Also, some money. Ironically, later we used the money that we were able to bring to the camp to wipe our bottoms. We simply didn't have any other paper. We tore ten-guilder notes into quarters and then we could use them four times. That was just fine, because it's not pleasant to have a dirty behind.

But in the train, of course, it was much different. We stood pressed close against each other. There were large cracks in the cars, and there were two grids of heavily rusted wire netting that let in some light. If by chance you landed next to such an air hole, you had some relief from the stench, but you could catch cold because it was so drafty.

The Frank family was with us in the car, but I only had contact with my sister. We protected each other against the shoving and the aggressiveness. The longer the trip lasted, the more belligerant people became. That's just the way it was. You couldn't get upset about that, because the kindest, gentlest people become aggressive when they've stood for a long time. And you get tired—so terribly tired—that you just want to lean against something, or if possible, even if only for a minute, to sit down on the straw. Then you sit on the straw and they step on you from all sides because you are sitting so low. All those feet and all that noise around you makes you aggressive—that goes without saying. And then you, too, push and hit. That's unavoidable, but Lientje tried to hold a small place clear for me and I tried to do the same for her. Near the bolts on the door, there was a hole through which you could look to see the landscape. If you were lucky enough to get a glimpse outside without being pushed away, you could breathe a little and put your thoughts in order.

By putting your thoughts in order, what I mean is that all the time you are busy thinking: How can I keep my feet on the ground? Can I sit down now for just a minute? How am I going to get past these legs? Watch out that Lientje doesn't push against that man, or he'll punch her. We weren't the only people who had these thoughts. Through that hole, you could see the marvelous landscape; we rode through magnificent cornfields. Everything was so peaceful and the weather was so wonderful that you forgot for a moment that you were sitting in a cattle car and that a war was going on.

We didn't realize where the train was going. We were told that we would go to Wolffenbüttel. We told each other that we'd never get that far since the Russians were practically in

Berlin. To go that far into Germany would be impossible. So we probably weren't going to Poland. Poland—to be going to Poland—that was our worst fear.

But standing on the loading platform in Auschwitz, we knew that we were in Poland.

We arrived in the dark. To start with, we went through the gates. The first thing we saw was the infamous sign: ARBEIT MACHT FREI. It was oppressively quiet. We passed many watchtowers, little houses surrounded by barbed wire, and high electric poles. Everyone knew immediately where we were. It was so insane—that moment of realization, Yes, this is an extermination camp. It was dreadful, horrible.

We were dead tired, because we had been on the train for four days. At that moment it began: "*Dallie, dallie, dallie* (hup, hup, hup), *alles hinaus,* (everybody outside), *schneller, schneller, schneller* (faster, faster, faster)." The station had a loud speaker. I still get gooseflesh whenever I'm in a station and I hear the voice that says, "Ladies and gentlemen, the train is out of service. Please go to the other track." But then, it was a voice that shouted, "*Alles austreten, alle Bagage hinlegen* (everybody out, put down your luggage), women to one side, men to the other side. Women and children who can't walk, go to the cars that are waiting for you."

The horrible effect of that very bright, dirty-looking neon light, a bluish light, and that gray sky above, more or less lit up by the neon lamps. And those little men in blue striped suits, who whispered, "*Ihr seid gesund. Lauf.* (You are healthy. Walk)." They were trying to warn us. We didn't understand any of it. We were too tired and too resigned and too far off balance to realize what was happening to us. Yes, it was a kind of nightmare, an inferno.

The names of a number of women were called, including Lientje and me. There was an SS officer who gathered these women together, checked the names again, and, in the midst of all that uproar, took us inside separately. Thus, as political prisoners, we got special treatment. We were put into groups of twenty-four or forty-eight—I don't remember anymore, and were washed and shaved separately. You didn't notice whether it was a man or a woman who shaved you. You were shaved below and under your arms. In our case, they seized us by the hair and cut it short, so we weren't shaved bald. We didn't know that there were others who were in fact shaved bald. But we were so shocked by the way they sent us from one person to the next. We were also tattooed. My number is very high, because I was among the last people to arrive in the camp. All of this lasted until it got light.

Then we were brought by an *Aufseherin* (a supervisor) to a place near the stone barracks. Later, we lived there. We were told to sit down. We were hungry, we were thirsty, we were terribly afraid. And then we had to shower, a tiny stream of water, which you went under in groups of five. We were so filthy and wanted so much to wash ourselves, and yet we got only a few drops of water. We didn't get a towel. We were driven through the huge room, where there was a terrible draft, and a garment was thrown at us.

Then we were awfully lucky, no doubt about that, because we got good wooden clogs. Luckily, we have small feet and there were clogs that were just the right size for Lientje and me.

We knew about the gas chambers. As soon as you arrived in Auschwitz, you knew about the gas chambers. How, I don't know. But we knew it. We saw that huge, black, smoky fire; we lived close by. We smelled the odor. You can never forget that.

But we didn't know yet that we had managed to escape going through the selection. There was a woman with us who was eighty-four years old. That was Luise Kautsky, the wife of Karl Kautsky, the well known Communist theorist and politician. She was the first who died—on that same day— while we sat there on the stones, in the burning sun. It was so hot and we were so thirsty. We each had one dress and a pair of clogs.

All of this was in Birkenau. The station was Auschwitz-

Birkenau. We had entered through Auschwitz and were taken directly to Birkenau. In Birkenau, we were quarantined immediately. We met a number of Dutch women who had been in the same transport with us. In the quarantine block where we were, there were all sorts of nationalities. There were Russian women, Italian women, even a couple of Norwegians or Danes. The Italian girls were very aggressive.

I remember something very nice about the French girls. They had been shaved completely bald. They found a little piece of glass and a small comb with three prongs. With that they combed their eyebrows, looking into the little mirror. Then they tied clothes around their heads and looked again to see if they weren't still a little bit elegant.

I find such things delightful. The Nazis tried to set countries and nations against each other and to attack and take away a person's best quality—his dignity. And so I find people like those French girls so marvelous—those girls who fixed up their eyebrows with a little dirt in order to look a little better—really what the French call *esprit,* the strength not to give up, not to knuckle under. Never.

———

In the camp it was as if you were being continually pounded by heavy hammers—on your heart, on your senses—until you were half stunned. You can try to protect what is dear to you. That's all that you can do. To thank the God of atheists on your bare knees that you are alone with your sister and there is no one else. And the mortifications you endure like lashes. The whole day you are on the alert, you can't do anything else, you keep on thinking about it. That's why we could never assimilate it. That's why we don't want it to ever happen to anyone— even our worst enemy.

It was a great, concentrated pressure or tension. Your entire humanity was injured. You could easily imagine lying there, dead, on the spot. If you were picked for work, if you had to

58

carry stones from the pits up to the top of the hill with a *Kapo* behind you, and you tried, like everyone else, to get that one stone that weighed less that was still so large, so that they would see that you were *schlepping,* then you felt so humiliated and so intensely violated that no words can describe it.

And then, that *Kapo* behind you. You're just a poor wretch and there's a *Kapo* wearing a splendid woolen angora sweater and a short skirt and high boots and magnificently piled up hair. She follows you with a whip in her hand. I won't say that they were all like that, but yes, we had good reason to hate those Polish *Kapos.* To this day I don't like angora sweaters.

Kapos were fellow prisoners. But they collaborated with the Germans. That's the only thing I can say about it. There were, of course, some very good *Kapos,* who helped fellow prisoners, but I wouldn't have wanted to be a *Kapo* in the camps where I was. In the last months that I was there, being a *Kapo* was no pleasant job. But you didn't always have a choice: sometimes you were selected and sometimes you could volunteer.

We were in quarantine at first, because an awful lot of people had scarlet fever, which was very contagious. Conditions in the sick barracks were so bad that you could die from even a simple throat infection. In spite of that the people who had scarlet fever were required to appear at the *Zählappell* (roll call). Those roll calls—they were also something frightful.

They began toward dawn—we didn't know what time it was, since we didn't have watches, but we could estimate that it was around 3:00–3:30 A.M. They yelled, *"Aus dem Block hinaus, Zählappell* (Out of the barracks, roll call)." And then they shook and rattled the bunks yelling at us all the time, and we jumped out of the bunks and ran outside. We were kicked out of the barracks by the women guards, the barrack *Kapos*. The *Kübel,* the cart in which we had peed and pooped, was driven away, and as we were leaving the barracks, we got a small amount of lukewarm coffee in our food pan—that was *moekefoek* (like dishwater). When you wanted to fix yourself up a little, you could use that to brush your teeth, even wash your hands, or take a sip—everything in that same little pan because you didn't have anything else.

And then, *"antreten in Fünfereihen* (line up in rows of five)." That meant that we had to form a square out of twenty-five people. You always tried to find your buddies so that you could lean on each other until the counting began. As soon as they started counting, you stretched out your arms and made sure that you were at the prescribed distance, so that it would be easier for them to count those blocks of twenty-five people. And they watched us, the *Scharführer,* and *Aufseherin,* and *Rottenführer,* and whatever they were all called. They came with dogs, firmly held on leashes. God help you if they got loose, because they bit, those nasty animals. I love dogs, but I have an everlasting terror of the huge curs like Great Danes—extremely vicious. They would calmly tear apart a baby before your eyes. Terrible creatures.

They came to count you and you all stood in squares of twenty-five. They walked along, peered in between the rows, and then went on. One thousand people—perhaps two thousand—stood there where they held roll call, until they had all been counted. When someone made a mistake or if their numbers didn't tally, then they would start all over again. We stood there for hours. It isn't at all amazing that people who were sick dropped dead. They had to be taken away—they were swept to the side—and now there were twenty-four instead of twenty-five, so the counting was repeated. You might say, as it were, that the counting continued until you dropped dead.

By nine or ten o'clock, or thereabouts, the roll call was finished. Then we could go inside and sometimes—and sometimes not—we got a little coffee and a piece of bread, baked very hard. For example, we got a loaf of *Kommissbrot* for six of us, which meant that each of us would get a one-inch piece of bread, and we would put a string or a piece of wood on it and slice it so that everyone got their portion. And if someone got half a centimeter an eighth of an inch more, there were angry looks. We sliced that one-inch strip of bread into thin slices so that we would have more tiny strips that would last longer.

We took that bread with us to work. You carried everything you owned with you—a small metal pan or bowl, an enamel cup, and a spoon. You were really rich if you had a spoon. You were even richer if you had a spoon and a knife. Lientje and I shared a knife, but each of us had a spoon.

There was a brisk trade in all sorts of things. We had received only a dress and a pair of shoes. During the day, it was dreadfully hot, but at night, it was terribly cold. Women who had gotten hold of two horse blankets tore each blanket into fourths and tied a piece under their skirts, which gave them the feeling that they were wearing pants. And later on, after a time, you got pants and stockings. You had to save your bread ration to get those. We divided one bread ration between the two of us and then, three days later, we bought first a pair of pants for one of us, and then a pair for the other. That way, we gradually dressed ourselves.

Directly after the roll call, some people were designated for the work parties, and those women took up positions apart from the others. But at the same time, those who had not been selected walked along with the stuff that they had obtained offering, for example, a pair of beautiful stockings in exchange for a piece of bread. That's how the trade worked. The legal tender was bread or an egg or a little salt. We all had terrible blisters on our tongues and very sore lips because of dryness and lack of vitamins. Thus, an onion was extremely valuable, as was salt. You'd do a lot to get that. Occasionally you could get a little sauerkraut; that was wonderful—that was a feast.

Lientje and I were together almost all the time. When Lientje had a high fever, I went with her to the sick-bay barracks, where they kept her. I was terribly frightened then. I stayed nearby and tried to go to her every chance I could get, because the worst that could happen to me would be to lose my sister.

After three days, I went to take her back to our barracks. She still hadn't recovered, but we took care of each other. We stood up for each other. Under all conditions.

We saw the Frank girls only briefly in Auschwitz. We weren't in the same barracks with them and we didn't come across them at work. We only met them again after the transport to Bergen-Belsen.

We did various things in Auschwitz. We worked in the *Weberei* (weaving mill), or folding plastic for airplanes. I still don't know what it was—a sort of transparent plastic. We took pieces of it and made belts, which we then bartered for other articles of clothing. I can still remember that we had to pull shoes apart, and what they did with them, I don't know. It was all work that made no sense.

They held selections on a regular basis, right after roll call. Instead of dispersing us, we were all ordered to go to the barracks, and then to come out, one by one, where death stood: Mengele and two others—who said, "You, to this side; you, to that side. You have *Krätze* (scabies), go to the *Krätzeblock* (scabies barracks)." Then you were lucky because it could just as well have been that you didn't go to the *Krätzeblock,* and we knew what that meant. We had seen that fire, that large, black, dirty fire.

We were naked when the selections were made. We were sent into the barracks to undress—we were completely naked, whether it rained or not, whether the sun was shining or not. Everyone, one by one, naked, out of the barracks. Mengele looked you over, from head to foot, and if you had pimples or a rash, then you could count on going to *that* side.

Fear, and not just of the selection, was constant. Selections were the norm. You can compare the situation to that of a mouse, who runs through the house, chased by everyone—the panic it feels when it can't find the hole it came out of. Fortunately, we didn't have to go through many selections.

In all the time we were in the camp, none of us menstruated.

We thought that they had put something in the food, but apparently that wasn't the case. It was simply that a woman living below subsistence level doesn't have a period. When I arrived at Birkenau, I was having my period. And after that, I didn't menstruate. I started again only after I had been home for half a year. Very strange.

In the barracks, we slept in bunks that were built in three levels. Each bunk was for two people, and theoretically six people could fit in each stack of three bunks. But that's not how it was, because instead of lying lengthwise, we lay across the breadth of the bunk, always five or six people. So we were terribly crowded. Those wooden frames creaked all the time from all that weight. If we were lucky there was some straw on the bunk, but otherwise we had only our blankets and we rested our heads on our fists. You would shove all your possessions tightly together—your comb; your spoon; and, if you had one, your knife; and your bowl—so that you could put them under your head. From time to time, if you kept something in your dish or in your mug, it would be stolen.

Not only was how we lay a problem, but so was sleeping in itself. It was a ghastly feeling to suddenly feel a hand under your head, or even worse, a rat, which might bite.

There wasn't only the physical contact between us—you were packed in like sardines in a can—but you still tried to talk with each other.

We didn't always talk of sticking together. We were set against each other and the closest relatives would begrudge each other a few potato peels. That wasn't meanness. That was hunger or nakedness. You became dehumanized in spite of yourself.

The conversation in the bunks was frequently about food. We also discussed world events. The women around us were, after all, politically conscious women, condemned for political crimes. In addition to fantasies about world revolutions, we would also imagine huge holiday feasts. When it became too noisy, during one of those holiday feasts, a *Kapo* would come along and say, "*Jetzt wird nicht gefressen, jetzt wird gestorben* (This is no time for eating; it's time to die)."

Because of the poor hygienic circumstances, we had to go to the *poepdoos* (poop box) together—a large, awful, stinking, smelly latrine. I still feel ill everytime I think of it because it was so horribly dirty. There were feces all over the place. You couldn't put your hands down anywhere, you could hardly put your feet down. Nevertheless you had to relieve yourself, because right afterward we were given the order to leave all together, and then you couldn't get away, and if you had to go, you had to do it in your pants if you had any. Now that never happened because our bowel movements were so slight that it wasn't worth the trouble. But urinating was annoying—then you walked straddle-legged.

There was always a lot of pushing at the water taps. It's a funny thing, but if you've brushed your teeth and washed your hands all your life, then you want to go on doing it and you have a real need to rinse your mouth with a little water. They grab your cup out of your hand, you have to push in order to get near the tap, and when you get there, you have to hold on tight to the tap because otherwise you won't get any water. You fight with all the other women. But you don't think about it, you just think, If I can just get that cloth wet, then I'll be able to wipe my hands. The only thing you think is, Well, damn it, if I can only go a bit farther so that Lientje can just get by; I'm a bit stronger than my sister. . . . It was always that way: the one took care of the other.

Ruth Feldman, who had been head nurse in the CIZ (Central Israelite Nursing Association) was with us in the barracks. She stepped forward and said that she was a nurse. And she wanted us to do so as well. So we did.

One of our *Kapos* once threw Ruth Feldman into the mess in that filthy latrine, and my feisty sister became so angry that she took off her clog and hit the *Kapo* on the head with it. The *Kapo* began to scream at the top of her lungs and tried to grab her,

64

but my sister was just a bit quicker and took off as fast as she could. There was a massive search for her, but she was able to hide someplace; if she had been caught, she would have been killed. Ruth was very grateful and said, "We have to try to stay together." But that simply didn't work out. We did indeed all end up in Bergen-Belsen, but at different times.

After we had reported as nurses in the final days of October, we were put on the transport to Bergen-Belsen.

In the beginning of November, we were called at roll call. They didn't say anything, but we sensed that something was going to happen. And it was true. They wanted to evacuate the camp because the Russians were getting closer. The camp was to be emptied, but we didn't know that. At the time we left Westerbork in cattle cars, we had had the feeling that we were being sacrificed, and so close before the liberation. And who would know where we had gone? After that, the hell of Auschwitz broke out all around us. And now we were in that hell and we were being transported again.

As far as we could see, it couldn't get any worse. Nothing could be worse than Auschwitz. We were picked out and told to go from one platform to the other, where we got bread and a few pots of water to take along. And then we were in the cattle cars again.

That trip lasted a terribly long time. There were air raid alarms and our train was fired on because the English probably thought it was a troop transport. And then the guards fled from the train, which we didn't know. We sat inside, and on the platforms we got fresh water and sometimes a piece of bread. We were allowed to go outside a couple of times; getting back on, you tried to be the last, in order to stay as close to the doors as possible. The two of us always tried to stay by the doors as much as possible. You could lie down in the straw along the sides so that you were protected on one side at least, and you could get some air through the crack.

We didn't know what was going on; we knew absolutely nothing. We had the feeling that we were aimlessly riding around. Until we stopped in Celle and a lot of people said, "Oh, we're going to Bergen-Belsen, now that's a good camp!" But disillusionment followed immediately. In the streaming rain and cold—oh, it was so cold—we had to walk. We stayed close together, two horse blankets over two thin girls. I can still see us walking those few kilometers from the Celle station to the Bergen-Belsen camp. We walked through the woods and breathed deeply . . . hmmm, woods, delightful. . . . We were surrounded by guards, and we passed the little town—the people saw us, us poor outcasts. No one lifted a finger to help us. And it rained and stormed and hailed.

Finally, we arrived at the camp on a moor with a bush here and there, and we sat down on a small hill, two girls pressed close together. But then another gray shape appeared and we threw the blankets off and called, "Oh, you're here too." It was Anne and Margot.

I have always assumed that they arrived on the same transport. There was a long, endless line entering the camp, and we sat on a little sand hill, as close together as possible, the blankets up to our noses, and then we suddenly saw those two girls also wrapped in blankets, and we thought, Well, they've gone through the same things we have. And then you are completely happy because you see that they've made it.

At that moment there was only happiness. Only the happiness of seeing each other. And we stayed together until we went into the tents. We also found the Daniëls girls whom we knew from Westerbork.

Maybe it was a "sister complex" that attracted our attention to the Frank girls and also to the Daniëls sisters. Sisters or mothers and daughters always tried to stay together. At that very moment, that feeling of togetherness, of having made it, was theirs as well. We had sort of motherly feelings for them because they were ten years younger than we were. On that same transport, we also found Sonja Lopes Cardozo and the daughter of Greetje van Amstel. We were reunited with quite a few of the young people, but that one moment, sitting on that little hill, we felt real joy because the children were still there. Now we felt at home. We took care, somehow, to see that the children stayed near us.

Large tents were put up hastily because, as we heard later, Bergen-Belsen had not counted on these transports at all. Beds were shoved into those army tents, one, two, three on top of each other. We were soaked and cold, and as soon as the tents were up, everyone ran to them. There was terrible elbowing and pushing to get inside the tents as quickly as possible. But we held back; at one point, the Frank girls were bickering about whether they should go in, and then they did.

We really weren't always nice to each other. Sometimes it almost came to blows. But the Frank girls decided to go on ahead of us. We waited a bit longer in the rain, and finally we were the very last ones to go into the tents. That was our usual strategy, and had been our salvation often. We had to scramble all the way to the top.

During the night there was a terrible storm, with thunder and lightning and hail and you name it—everything that the weather gods could produce came down on us and shook and tore at the tents. Two or three tents, including ours, collapsed.

In each tent, there were a couple of hundred people. A lot of people were injured and, I think, even a few died. We were fortunate. Because we had crept up high and the canvas was torn, we were able to get out. But there was terrible devastation. And in the morning, it was as if there had been a shipwreck. People and piles of wreckage everywhere—moaning and pain.

We didn't find the Frank girls until a few days later. We were transferred to wooden and stone barracks. We stayed the longest in the wooden barracks. Naturally, we went to look for people we knew. Not the Frank girls in particular, just acquaintances. We found quite a few, people with whom we had talked and had contacts, with whom we had been together, and with whom we once had a party, up on our bed in Auschwitz.

That party was for *Sinterklaas,* Christmas, Hannukah, and

New Year's—we celebrated them all at once. We brought together all the people we knew and trusted for that.

To celebrate the important holidays, we saved bread, everything that we could collect and beg. I know that Lientje sang for the *Blockälteste.* In those barracks, there weren't only *Kapos,* but also a *Blockälteste,* the authority in charge of the barracks, who was supposed to ensure a fair distribution of things, and whose fair distribution consisted of: First me, then me, then me, and then a little for you, and a little for you, and then the rest of the barracks.

Lientje earned a few pieces of bread with her singing. We saved those. We saved everything we could get our hands on. That evening, we celebrated Christmas, New Year's, and Hannukah. That night, we all sat up on the beds in one of the stone barracks and sang together.

There were a lot of Hungarians in the barracks. A great many Hungarians were gassed.

At the same time that our transport had arrived in Auschwitz-Birkenau, a very large transport came with Hungarian men and women and gypsies. And at that time, the furnaces burned continuously. That grimy, black, stinking smoke, which produced cinders.

In every barracks in Bergen-Belsen, there were Hungarians and Czechs, all women, because I'm talking about the women's camp. There were Russian women, too, I think. And we sat there, up on our bed, with all kinds of things to eat, which we didn't eat—we just snacked—and we sang. I'd like to tell a remarkable story about that.

We were all trying our best not to cry, although we were all thinking of our loved ones. The Dutch girls sang practically non-stop: *"Het karretje, dat op de zandweg reed* (The cart that rode on the sandy road)." Briefly, that song is about a coachman who goes to the horse standing in front of the cart. He says, "You will take me home my friend, my friend, you will take me home," and so forth. It was one of the dramatic, sentimental songs that we had learned at school. In addition to *"Het karretje op de zandweg,"* we sang all sorts of songs: *"Het zonnetje gaat van ons scheiden* (The sun is going to leave us)," *"Een moeder bukt zich voor God den Heer om haar avond* (A mother bows before the Lord in the evening)," *"Kling klang het klokje* (Ding dong the clock)," *"Het avondgebed* (Evening prayer)." They were all very sentimental school songs that we sang. That evening we sang them all.

The Czechs were very testy because the Hollanders kept on singing—they just wouldn't stop singing, and then they shouted, "Quiet, quiet, we want to sing a Dutch song." It was so impressive that suddenly all our bottled-up tensions were gone and we all began to cry. But we wept quietly—it was a liberation, I have to say. They sang in harmony, *"Constant had een hobbelpaard zonder kop of zonder staart, zo reed hij de kamer rond, zo maar in zijn . . . [blote kont]. Constant had een hobbelpaard* (Constant had a hobby horse, without a head and without a tail, so he rode around the room . . . [bare assed])." And we sat there crying. Isn't that typical? It is so Dutch to keep on going, to keep your grief to yourself, and to control yourself, and then to have someone else break the tension, and suddenly be freed.

The next day, SS-man Muller was furious because he hadn't been able to go home for Christmas and New Year's. Dead drunk, he tried to whack us out of our upper bunks. He thrashed the sides of the beds with his whip. We resisted, tooth and nail, pressing ourselves against the bunks, and he couldn't get us. When it was necessary, we defended ourselves quite well!

The Frank girls and the Daniëls girls and Sonja Lopes Cardozo were with us then; we squatted on our upper bunk; above us was the sloped roof. It was a memorable experience that we all felt deeply—an experience that you never forget.

One day, Lientje went out alone and when she came back, she said, "Janny, come with me for a minute." And we walked to a small barracks and there—to our great amazement—we saw only Dutch women: Sister Asscher, Mrs. Levie, Mrs. de Zoet, who died near us, Roosje Pinkhof, and Carrie Vos. They were people who had been on the diamond *Sper* (the list of people exempted from the transport because they were in the diamond business). And they were threatened by the camp commanders in the *Austauschlager* (the exchange camp for people designated to go to Palestine).

All the people were subjected to the most vicious sorts of threats in order to make their fight for survival even more difficult and to create even more tension. One punishment—a very common one—was, for example, to have to kneel in front of the barracks with a stone in your hands. No one could talk to you or you would be beaten. You were also beaten if you turned your head—and you had to stay there for hours. A lot of people died that way. It was not easy to stay alive; it was easier to die. It was easy to contrive something in order to die. And if you had no other ideas, it was even simpler just to walk into the barbed wire. Countless people walked into the electrified barbed wire. I don't think that's a secret. People made their farewells and walked into the barbed wire (in Auschwitz). Bergen-Belsen didn't have electrified barbed wire. Maybe it was there, but not where we were.

These women—there were only a handful—had lost their *Sper.* They had had to deliver diamonds everyday or they would be transported. And their men were transported, too.

Those women and children were pitiful. Awful. They had been in the camp much longer and they had endured many privations. They had remained with their relatives throughout and had stayed on their feet because their families were nearby. Now that suddenly fell apart. We immediately began to help them. They were sick and helpless. We started by getting water and trying to wash them.

In Bergen-Belsen, it was, in fact, possible to wash yourself. We carried water in pots and cups and the little pans we ate from, so that we could wash clothes once in a while. It was very primitive, but it worked. As nurses, we were allowed to go into the dispensary—we had to report our people who were sick, didn't we? So we could move about a bit more freely. Which meant that we could do other things. I stole handfuls of very smelly stuff to get rid of bedbugs and fleas.

Then Lientje said, "Shall we ask tonight whether we can stay in that barracks?" And it worked. So we moved to the small barracks with the Dutch women. Sister Asscher died there, but we nursed her children, Jopie and Bram, back to health and got them back to Holland.

There was a large group of Dutch children there and the Nazis didn't know if they were Jewish or not. They might have been *Mischlingen* (children from mixed marriages) and questions might come up about them later. So the authorities took special care of those children.

All of us, especially the young women, would go to see the children regularly to tell them a few simple children's stories. Normally they heard only screaming *Aufseherinnen* (supervisors) and *Kapos,* who only wanted to further their own interests through the children. We clipped the nails and, once in awhile, the hair of the tiny one. We acted toward them like anxious mothers. Fortunately, the majority of the children were taken by the Red Cross to Eindhoven soon after the liberation. I've had word from some of them, but I lost sight of most of them. Besides, I think that most of the children didn't want any more contact because they wanted to forget as much as possible, and that is for the best.

I know that Anne and Margot also involved themselves with the children and that we did our best to help them. Not only Anne and Margot, but also the other girls we knew went regularly to provide them with a little balance and sometimes a little culture.

It is very important sometimes to disengage yourself from the mess in which you find yourself, to shut your eyes and turn yourself off. I have to say that I myself, when we were removing dead people's bodies, stood in front of that stinking pit many times and turned around and looked at that magnificent starry sky and said, "Oh God, if you really exist, how could you let this happen?"

We took care of the children as well as possible, but we never had enough time. We ran ourselves crazy, and to make matters worse, Lientje got sick. She got typhus fever. Mrs. Levie was one of the first ones in our barracks to get typhus. Another nurse, Mrs. Bronkhorst, was with us in the barracks and helped with the sick. Sometimes, I can't remember the names, but there were indeed people who survived the typhus. Mrs. Levie didn't survive and Mrs. de Zoet didn't survive.

As nurses, we had to count the sick people and report them during the *Zählappell;* we were now in a somewhat better position. In Auschwitz-Birkenau, they would go to the infirmary barracks, but in Bergen-Belsen, the infirmaries were so full that those who were ill stayed in their own barracks. Ours was this kind of barracks. We had our hands full, but we continued to look for acquaintances. Roosje Pinkhof was with us in the barracks and Carrie Vos, too. The Daniëls girls came to see us regularly.

I didn't visit the headstrong Frank girls very often. When we wanted to find them in that total chaos of Bergen-Belsen, we couldn't because their barracks had been moved.

It was chaos, no one knew anymore where anyone was; it was a terrible mess, but the counting continued. . . . Everybody still stood at the roll call place and when someone had escaped or was lost, the counting went on for hours.

I had a white band on my arm, and when a group of girls would go to get water, I would carry the pot because there were thieves who would take the water. Sometimes they would grab it right out of your hands. We stood a long time at the pump before we got any water. The water supply was irregular. Eating was very irregular. There were Red Cross packages, but we never got them. I know that Mrs. Boissevain went to a lot of trouble to send us Red Cross packages (from Holland), but they never arrived. The Asscher children did get Red Cross packages once.

Because of our duties, we had access to the SS pharmacy where we could surreptitiously steal things, like aspirin, salve against lice, and other medications. We distributed what we got, also to the Frank girls, who weren't in our barracks.

There was no gas chamber in Bergen-Belsen, at least not within our range. But there was an enormous pit and we dragged our dead there. I always have a little trouble with the word "corpse." I never think of a corpse as a dead human being.

Young girls who were still strong, such as Roosje and Carrie, and whoever else could, also carried dead people wrapped in blankets, to the pit. But we wanted to keep those blankets and, in a manner of speaking, they were shaken empty into that large, stinking pit. The smell was indescribable. And then the birds that flew down into it . . .

Anne had typhus. I had typhus myself, but right up to the end, I was able to stay on my feet. I took only aspirin since I had a raging fever. There was too much to do. Lientje was sick. Water had to be fetched. I always tried to first make sure that Lientje had water; that wasn't egotistical, that was normal; I thought that I had the right to favor my sister. And in fact, I wouldn't have wanted to come back to Holland if my sister hadn't survived. Only on the day of liberation did I finally collapse. But up to then I kept myself on my feet, in spite of being sick.

Anne was sick, too, but she stayed on her feet until Margot died; only then did she give in to her illness. Like so many others, as soon as you lose your courage and your self-control . . .

We did what we could, but there was no question of real nursing. The nursing only consisted of giving the sick some water to drink and, if you had the chance, washing them off a little. In the first place, the most we could do for people with open, gaping wounds was to use a paper bandage. There wasn't anything else, no nursing supplies. An awful lot of people had frostbite. When you stood, for hours, at the *Zählappell,* then there were black toes, noses, and ears—jet black.

The women who were ill, including the Frank sisters, were

in the regular barracks, not in the infirmary barracks. They were once in the infirmary barracks, but then one got another of them out, just as we had done. Our help wasn't enough, but we couldn't do more than we did. Above all, Lientje was already sick then. I had, of course, told the children stories, and when Lientje was sick, I brought Brammetje and Jopie Assher to her and thought up games for them. Lientje did as much as as I did, no mistake about it. But it was simply a battle. Mrs. Scheermes died in that barracks, with her baby—who was still alive—in her arms. Nursing gave us the opportunity to offer help to the Frank children, and to others as well.

At a certain moment in the final days, Anne stood in front of me, wrapped in a blanket. She didn't have any more tears. Oh, we hadn't had tears for a long time. And she told me that she had such a horror of the lice and fleas in her clothes and that she had thrown all of her clothes away. It was the middle of winter and she was wrapped in one blanket. I gathered up everything I could find to give her so that she was dressed again. We didn't have much to eat, and Lientje was terribly sick but I gave Anne some of our bread ration.

Terrible things happened. Two days later, I went to look for the girls. Both of them were dead!

First, Margot had fallen out of bed onto the stone floor. She couldn't get up anymore. Anne died a day later. We had lost all sense of time. It is possible that Anne lived a day longer. Three days before her death from typhus was when she had thrown away all of her clothes during dreadful hallucinations. I have already told about that. That happened just before the liberation.

I would like to mention that I had worked together with Hungarian Communists. Two Hungarian girls came up to me one morning at roll call and said, "You're in that small barracks, aren't you? Would you do something for us? We have to go to the *Entlausung* (delousing center). Would you keep our suitcase for us?"

"Yes, of course," I said. And I hid it in Lientje's bed. She lay on top of it. I always had Lientje go and lie down as soon as possible after the roll call. Actually, that wasn't allowed during the day. Only those who were severely ill could do that. When the girls returned from the *Entlausung,* they wanted to know what I would like as a reward, because everything suddenly had a barter value.

But I said, "Don't be silly, you don't have to pay for that."

And they answered, "Listen, we are forming a large group of five-woman cells. We would very much like to have you participate."

Those women met in the dark near the corpse pit, because the Nazis didn't go there. And then the work would be distributed. The women were in different work parties all over the camp; five were in the writing room, five were in the potato kitchen, etc. They tried to do what we did, namely, to ensure that the women in the barracks were well treated and taken care of after work. I bandaged frozen feet and cut off frozen toes—yes, that was simply the reality. They gave me the opportunity to stay longer in the SS pharmacy and showed me the places where certain remedies were kept which you could hide in your pants or whatever you had on, and with which one could then help.

At a certain point, those girls said that the liberation was close at hand. They often provided extra morsels, such as a piece of raw onion or a piece of raw turnip. So we exchanged things with each other. Then a messenger said that it was possible to escape and to provide us with a little gold that they had taken from the *Bekleidungskammer* (dressing room). So we all got a little sack around our neck that had a few gold coins to be used if we were able to escape. Nothing came of that because the English were already very close.

The English detoured around the camp when they heard that the camp was filled with illness and infection. They didn't dare to go in; they waited for the medical corps, which came shortly thereafter. In the meantime, the Nazis evacuated the camp as quickly as possible. That's why there were the forced marches out of Bergen-Belsen.

All people who were healthy had to walk. The Hungarians said, "Try to get out of the camp because the camp is mined; they want to blow the camp up before the English get here." Those were IPAs (reports from the Israelite Press Bureau). But IPAs were always scare reports.

At one point, there were a lot of air raid alarms. Then suddenly everything was quiet, the Nazis were gone. We hadn't had anything to eat that day, but we weren't surprised at that. The Nazis were gone! That evening, when we realized that the Nazis were gone, there was an orgy. You can't imagine what that was like. There was a mountain of turnips as high as a house. And in less time than it takes me to tell about it, that mountain had disappeared. The guards' barracks were set on fire. Pictures of Hitler and his cronies, with their eyes poked out, were waved around. It was a complete orgy. I was already sick. So sick that I could hardly move anymore. At that point, the Nazis came back. They were all wearing white bands on their arms. In the morning, they whistled and screamed and there was a roll call. We thought we had been liberated, and it wasn't so. Grumbling, we went to the roll call place. I had to drag myself, with my raging fever. Total anarchy broke out in the camp. there were fires everywhere. The few soldiers who had stayed behind shot at anything that moved. So you could have been shot dead, even in the final moments.

The craziest things happened. People who put on parts of SS uniforms were killed by others who thought that they were Nazis. The craziest things—I can't describe how crazy it was.

Jozef Kramer, the commandant, stepped onto a small pedestal and said, "*Kommen sie her, kommen sie näher . . .* (Come here, come here), come closer, come stand around me, *meine Damen* (dear ladies)." People jeered and yelled. There wasn't any roll call because he wanted to say that he was going to turn the camp over to the English, who stood right behind the fences. That was the last roll call.

I saw Jozef Kramer being arrested by the English. That gave me enormous satisfaction. I saw how he was thrown into a jeep and was kicked in the ass, and how the stripes were pulled off his uniform and how the white bandage on that coward's arm was ripped off and how he was shackled like a prisoner and taken away in that jeep. And then I collapsed.

I regained consciousness as two little fat men were cutting the clothes away from my body. I sputtered, "No, no, I'll be too cold." And I heard something, but the buzzing in my head was much louder. I was picked up, and without any clothes on, wrapped up in a blanket, put on a stretcher, and brought to a large hall. I thought that I was in hell. There were kerosene burners everywhere. Swiss nurses began to wash me. There was nothing else around me, just those two nurses. who were looking at me. They spoke with each other, but I couldn't understand anything because I had such a buzzing in my head. The only thing I said was, "Please don't cut my hair off because my husband won't want me back with a bald head."

And they didn't do that. They did clean me up, but they didn't cut off my short hair.

After that, I was brought to the big SS hospital that was on the grounds of Bergen-Belsen. There I finally began to realize that the liberation had come. That was in the large SS Red Cross station. But in my feverish fantasies, Bob and the children were with me. I didn't give a second's thought to Lientje. I was only busy thinking about my thirst and why I didn't get something to drink. And then Bob gave me a bottle of lemonade, and then the children came and said, "Go on sleeping, go on sleeping, we drank it up." And then I cried, "Bob, the children are bothering me, can you see to it that they don't bother me?"

When I came to, a Swiss nurse sat on my bed and said, "Now, you're going back to Bob." Then I thought vaguely, "How does she know that?"

I couldn't move my hands, and I could hardly open my mouth. But within two days, everything was much better.

A nurse sat on my bed and said, "You're going back to Amsterdam."

I asked immediately, "Lientje, where is Lientje?"

"Who is Lientje?"

Me again: "My sister."

"Oh," she said, "I don't know."

Then I thought, Why should I go on talking, I'm going to die. I just wanted to die, and then I finally began to cry. The tears ran down my cheeks—I can still feel those tears. I couldn't wipe them off because I couldn't lift my arms. The tears rolled over me—it was such complete unhappiness. Very strange, very sad. I wanted to die; I didn't want to go on living, because I didn't know where Lientje was. And after several days of having been fed intravenously, I didn't want to eat. I just cried.

The nurse went to the end of the ward and stood there whispering with the doctor. She probably said, "She is in bad shape because she wants to find her sister." I heard her say, "The sister's probably dead."

The doctor came and sat down with me. He was an Irishman, a red-headed Irishman, Jim, who immediately said, "Call me Jim. Where do you come from?"

"Amsterdam."

"Do you have any family?" He had a way of asking only questions that would require short answers. "Was your sister with you? Do you know where she is?"

"No."

"Listen, I promise you that I'll go and look for her. But now you have to eat something."

A few hours later, I think, I suddenly heard Lientje's voice. It was a very crazy reunion.

There was an office behind the infirmary barracks where I lay. Lientje came there every day. She had stayed in the barracks for people who weren't ill and was looking for me. She was convinced that I wasn't dead and said, "I'll find her." She was already booked on the first plane to go to Eindhoven. The plane that the children went on. She had already made friends and said that she needed seats for two people. "My sister is here someplace, and I'm going to find her." A faith in God—fortunately, it was rewarded.

Lientje walked along the glass windows for the hundredth time on her way to the office to ask if I had been found, and I heard her voice. And after that, she came through the ward and I raised my hand as high as I could and she saw me. Both of us broke down and cried.

She told me—I couldn't understand everything she said—that we were going home on the plane. "I told them who we are. As former resistance workers, a great deal will be done for us. But I'm taking you with me; you have to get out of bed. Because otherwise, I can't take you with me."

Then she got two strong girls from her barracks and they carried me there. There I lay, on a lower bunk, crying uncontrollably. They tried to give me something to eat; they put a piece of bread in my mouth and I almost choked. In the meantime, we had noticed that there were ambulance jeeps in the area. Lientje went to the special diet kitchen and asked if she could get something for her sick sister. Then they asked where the sick sister came from and she said, "I got her out of that barracks."

"Oh," they said, "Oh, she is still contagious." And they took me back.

Jim promised me that I had to stay only a few days. As soon as I was well, he would see to it that Lientje and I would go to Holland together. But the plane left without either of us.

I think it was about a week later when we left. We rode in trucks; it was a long journey. We met so many people. We drove back to Holland in short stages—eighteen to twenty-five miles a day. On the way Lientje almost died from taking two pills that I had gotten from Jim, the doctor, because I had heart problems. She had to have her stomach pumped out at a hospital.

79

Slowly, we approached Soltau. There we were taken to a hangar, an airplane hangar. While we were standing there talking, a hatch just opened up. There was a provision room under it, full of raisins, bars of almond paste, marzipan, and so forth. We were actually very well taken care of by the English, but this was something that wasn't expected at all. In no time all the people who were sleeping there on the straw hauled out the marzipan and divided it among themselves. We were perfect in organizing that. And a couple of hours later, the commandant, together with the Dutch officer who was there, also a commandant—they were all commandants; we all had a "commandant complex" because we had been in a camp and in a camp you had a commandant! Anyway, the commandant came with a number of soldiers to look for the marzipan and the raisins, because they were actually intended for—I don't know if it was Easter or Whitsunday—but it was all for a special occasion, and each of us was to get a share. But all of us said very innocently that we didn't know where it was. Someone opened his mouth and blabbed that we did know about the supply of sweets. And then someone else thought that it should be fairly divided. We didn't think so. We didn't think that it had to be fairly shared. We had already taken our share and we were sitting on it, under the straw, and we took it with us to Holland.

A day later, we had to wait for the delegation from the Dutch government that was to receive us in Enschede. But they never showed up. What was most impressive is that we crossed the border in the trucks and got Dutch flags, which we unfolded the moment the frontier barrier was opened. We all sang the "Wilhelmus" (the Dutch national anthem) at the top of our voices, with tears running down our cheeks. Communists or not, we had returned to set foot on the soil of our fatherland. When we arrived at the Drienderweg, there were dozens of children with little flags in their hands who cried "Hooray." But that wasn't meant for us, but for the trucks that were coming over the border, bringing the children chocolate and sweets. We didn't have anything at all to offer; we only had ourselves. That was a very big disappointment. A little sobered, we were brought to the bathhouse on the Driender-weg. There wasn't any delegation to welcome us. And for the—I don't know—hundredth time we had to be deloused. At each place we stopped on that trip home, we were deloused, had our clothes inspected, and were questioned once again. In the first place, it was to prevent bringing in any infectious diseases. In the second place, it was to unmask people who traveled with us pretending to have been in the resistance; the English handled that very well. In Soltau, the last stop before the border, they hauled a number of people out and turned them over to ex-prisoners to be delivered. We left them un-scathed; we didn't do anything to them.

In Enschede, we each received a guilder. Lientje and I bought a herring with it—delicious. We were put up in a dirty old school building. We protested about that. The next day we were brought to a better internment center. The commandant there was one of the Boissevain boys, Harry, who had worked with my brother-in-law, Jan. He knew me and told me he would see to it that we got to Amsterdam quickly.

The first evening in Holland we got turnips to eat!!!

My sister is a very diligent enthusiastic person, and she immediately wanted to entertain the repatriots; she found a piano somewhere and wanted to practice on it. I was up in my room. Harry brought me downstairs and said, "Don't say any-thing to the other women; you are going to Amsterdam. Now keep your mouth shut, because it could start a rebellion here."

Then we left by car with a dentist who was looking for a relative. The roads were barricaded, because there were a lot of infectious illnesses in North Holland and thru-traffic wasn't permitted. But this man had gotten a special permit to go to North Holland. Four people went along: Lientje and I, a woman from Harderwijk, an old woman—we thought she was very old, she was sixty-four—and a young woman from Hilversum. That old woman had sheltered English pilots and had been in a house of detention. In Harderwijk, we had a party. The woman from Hilversum found her house empty; her husband and the children—they had had Jewish children in the house— had disappeared.

The closer we got to Amsterdam, the more restless we got. We really didn't know what it would be like in Amsterdam. We had two contact addresses. One was the address of Haakon and Mieke Stotijn at 25 Johannes Verhulststraat. We drove there, but no one was home. There was, however, a note on the door that read, "In case Lientje and Janny come by, go three houses farther up, to Jopie Bennet's, where there is a long letter for you."

We picked it up and it was a letter from my brother-in-law Eberhard in which he wrote, "Bob is living with both children at 101 Amstel, and I am living in Oegstgeest with Mr. Blom."

We raced to 101 Amstel. Because we didn't know exactly where it was, we began by the Berlagebrug and drove along the Amstel. I did nothing but sob.

Lientje—I had scolded Lientje so often—she now scolded me for everything under the sun, she said, "Have you gone mad? Now finally we're going to Bob and the children and you sit there and cry. What is this, are you nuts?"

In any case we crossed the bridge and Lientje called out, "Yes, that's the house. Those curtains hanging there are like the ones you had in the Hague." And I didn't dare to turn around to look. The car stopped and Lientje flew out and ran inside, but I didn't get out, because I couldn't deal with it anymore. . . .

Bob ran out of the house and lifted me out, carried me inside. Lientje stood on the stoop and yelled, "I have to go to Oegst-geest, because Eberhard is in Oegstgeest with Katinka and I have to go to Oegstgeest." My son Rob stood on the stoop, calling, "Children, children, come here everybody, I have my own mother back, I really have my own mother. Papa, I said that she would come back, Papa, I said that all along; Mama promised me that she would come back; see, Mama keeps her promises." That was the homecoming.

I had a husband and two children, I was rich. I knew what others could expect, most of whom wouldn't come back. I went to the SOL, the forerunner of the Foundation '40-'45, the Solidarity Foundation. That organization was set up early, at the beginning of the Second World War by a number of people who felt a responsibility for the women whose husbands had been arrested. We had people appointed paymasters, including Rhijnvis Feith and Hans Voorhoeve in the Hague. In the winter of 1941, when I was still in the Hague, we collected food in order to provide something extra to those women whose husbands had been picked up.

In the first days after the liberation, I went to that Solidarity Foundation. I knew Trees Lemaire, who was then a member of Parliament for the SDAP (Social Democratic Workers Party). Bob had even briefly been in hiding in Trees Lemair's house; she was a good old friend of ours. Trees and her mother, Marie, gave me all the clothes they could find in their closets.

In those days, I also went immediately to the Red Cross to look at the lists that showed who had survived and who had died. And I put a cross next to the names of those who I knew had actually died.

I also put a cross next to the names of Anne and Margot. Much later, in the summer of 1945, a tall, thin, distinguished man stood on the sidewalk. He looked through our window and Bob opened the door, because he often protected me. In the beginning, I had to deal so much with family members whom I had to tell that their sons, daughters, and husbands would not be coming back. That was often unbearable. And it was especially difficult to deal with because I had survived and had come back.

And there stood Otto Frank. He asked if I knew what had happened to his two daughters. I knew, but it was hard to get the words out of my mouth. He had already heard from the

Red Cross, but he wanted to have it confirmed. He had also been to see Lientje. Lientje, who had been terribly ill, had rented a small house in Laren. He had gone to Laren and spoken with Lientje and Eberhard. And I had to tell him that . . . that his children were no more.

He took it very hard. He was a man who didn't show his feelings openly, he had tremendous self-control. He was a tall, thin, aristocratic man. Later, we saw him frequently. By a remarkable chance, Anne's manuscript (her diary) was found at Annie Romijn's. And Annie Romijn was in our circle of friends. That's really amazing. And later he came often. He always stayed at the Hotel Suisse on Kalverstraat, where my relatives from Brussels always stayed. I always found that so nice.

———

Assimilating these experiences is very difficult for me. Actually, I never have. For days and nights on end, I talked Bob's ears off. Every time the rage would leap up into my throat. But you can't assimilate it; the only thing is that it becomes a bit farther removed from you.

I want to repeat, I have told this because I want to make it very clear to a large number of people that all discrimination—whatever form it takes—is evil and that the world can go to pieces because of it. Actually, literally, go to pieces. Discrimination against someone because of his skin color or his ears or his hair, or God knows what—we can all die from that. It only takes one person to say, "He isn't as good as I am, because he has. . ." You can fill in the rest.

If I had been able to assimilate it all, then it wouldn't be so difficult. We have learned to live with it and we have perhaps been able to put a little distance between what happened and the present. But it was such an unreal and such a catastrophic time in my life, that there is no question of its assimilation. A tiny movement, a small noise, or the smell of burned food—

and I'm right back, where I was. You can talk about it, but no one can ever relieve you of it. In this respect, the Fascists achieved a worldwide victory. We have to make sure that it will never happen again.

RACHEL VAN AMERONGEN-FRANKFOORDER

Rachel van Amerongen–Frankfoorder.

I had known Rachel and her husband, Eddy van Amerongen, the former director and editor of the Nieuw Israëlitisch Weekblad (New Israelite Weekly), for several years before a close mutual friend told me about Rachel's concentration camp experiences.

In 1950, Rachel, Eddy, and their two children settled in Israel. They spend virtually every summer in the Netherlands, in order to escape the heat in Israel. The Netherlands has always been an important place for Rachel—not only because of the cool summers there.

When I called her and cautiously asked whether it was true that she had seen Anne Frank in the concentration camp, it was as if I had opened a door that had been locked for a long time. It turned into a long telephone call during which she told me many important things about her experiences. Only later I learned that she rarely talked about her past. "When I returned to Holland, we were a miserable lot of women. And no one was very interested in what we had gone through. We were dead. Written off. So I decided never to talk about it. Even to my children."

Her decision to open up proved to be a catharsis, a totally unexpected liberation. "It was much more difficult to remain silent. Because it always comes back, the memory. Now I'm telling you things from the depth of my soul. I don't want to make it a big drama. But it is."

Our contact, which had already been considerable before this period, intensified during the production of the documentary. The filming of Rachel's account took place in the summer of 1987.

Rachel's first contact with Otto and Anne Frank was in Westerbork. In Bergen-Belsen, she was in the same barracks as Anne and Margot. In February 1945, she was transported to Raguhn. Finally, she was liberated from the Theresienstadt concentration camp.

Rachel van Amerongen– Frankfoorder

I was born in the Dutch-Israelite Hospital on the Nieuwe Kei-zers Canal in 1914 and I grew up on the other side of the river IJ in Amsterdam-North, where we lived on Nachtegaalstraat. I had a protected childhood in a socialist environment. My father was a typographer. I had two brothers, who died misera-bly in a concentration camp with their wives, as did my par-ents. I was always aware that Nazism in Germany was very bad for Jews and that to fall into their hands meant the end.

I did resistance work during the war. I was able to secure ration coupons through a connection at the Exchange building on the Damrak. I delivered those coupons to people who had gone into hiding—Jews and non-Jews.

On the way from Rotterdam to Amsterdam, I was arrested on the train by a Dutch SS man. I can still see him before me—short, with red hair and a red mustache. I could pick him out anywhere. The Germans weren't sure why I had been arrested, but he knew for certain that my identification card was not completely on the up and up; he was an expert in those matters, as it turned out.

First I was brought to the police station at the Central Station, and afterward I spent about three weeks in the prison on the Amstelveenseweg.

All the prisoners were taken from there to Westerbork, where we were put in overalls right away, got clogs, and then were taken to an "S" barracks—the punishment barracks. The men were shaved bald and had to wear a cap. It was terrible because you were afraid all the time about what was happening with your family, for they didn't hear anything from you anymore.

I worked on batteries for the first few days. After a transport left Westerbork they needed women to work at the internal service near the entrance of the camp, and I went to work there. That meant scrubbing, cleaning the toilets, and handing out overalls and clogs when new transports arrived.

From time to time, people were brought to us who had received nothing to eat in the work barracks. They came in very weak. All their mess tins were brought in and we had to dish out the food. Afterward, you were free to speak with the people. This work assignment—the internal service—was very popular, but I myself didn't make any special effort to get work there. Our crew consisted of six women. Among them was Mien Vitali, the Italian chimney sweep's wife.

I met Leo Beek in the "S" barracks. He had been my manager in the Bijenkorf (a department store in Amsterdam), where I had worked for thirteen years. A very tall, good-looking man, unapproachable and haughty. But now he was disfigured, walking with difficulty in the wooden clogs, and he wasn't so tall anymore.

He had been arrested despite the fact that he was married to a non-Jew. His wife was Cissy van Marxveldt, the famous writer of books for young girls. Nevertheless, that was not enough to save him, because he had been working on a military plan—he had a very high rank in the service—a liberation plan for the Netherlands. He was arrested because of that and landed in the punishment barracks in Westerbork, where I met him. Despite the dismal circumstances, he was awfully happy to see me, and I was happy, too.

He had been a man whom, if you ran into him in the hall in the Bijenkorf, you would avoid looking at because he had such a stern appearance. Now that was completely gone. Now he was as friendly and down-to-earth as possible. Alas, a few weeks later he was shot.

There were other people there I knew. Leo Cohen, former superintendent of police in Amsterdam, was a very good friend of mine. Later, after the war, he came to visit us. We still stay in close touch with his widow.

In the "S" barracks I also met the Frank family: Otto Frank, his wife, and two children. Otto Frank came up to me with Anne and asked if Anne could help me. Anne was very nice and also asked me if she could help me. She said, "I can do everything; I am very handy." She was really so sweet, a little older than she was in the photo that we've all seen, gay and cheerful. Unfortunately, I had no say in the matter. I sent her to the people in charge of the barracks. I couldn't do more than that.

After a few days, I think that she, with her sister and mother, landed in the battery department, because almost all of the women went there, with the exception of one person, Lien van Os, who worked for the commandant. She was an enormous woman who wore blue overalls. She was picked up every morning, and she had to clean the commandant's car in the garage. Later she was one of the first in the camp to die of typhus.

Everyone was divided into work groups; I think that people were eager to work in the inside service. That is actually quite logical. You didn't have to go outside—in the rain or in the mud. Cleaning batteries wasn't so pleasant, nor was cleaning toilets, but people preferred doing the latter. I think Otto Frank was eager to arrange that for Anne. That's the reason that he came to me with Anne—not with his wife and not with Margot. I think that Anne was the apple of his eye. Otto Frank was an especially nice and friendly man. You sensed that he had known better times. It was a lovely family.

I didn't see Otto Frank and his family again in Westerbork. I thought that they had been transferred to the *vrije* (free) barracks. People thought that it was very important to get out of the punishment barracks. I didn't think that it was so important, because you were imprisoned wherever you were. I never tried to get out of the punishment barracks because I thought, What then? I had, after all, seen that people from the free barracks were just as likely to go on the transport. We did hear about people who went to Bergen-Belsen, a camp with a good reputation—and to go to Theresienstadt, that was the absolute pinnacle. I was indifferent about that. I only wanted one thing: freedom.

It was always terrible when a transport arrived. Then you had to put the people's clothes into sacks. Under the supervision of Abraham van Witsen, the sacks full of clothes were brought to a warehouse and stored on racks. When people were put on a transport, you had to go to get their clothes and give them back—always a horrible job. All of that was very, very bad. Unpleasant confrontations. You knew, very well, where they were going, and that it always meant death.

I saw that clearly, and I think most people realized it. No one dared to say it out loud. But everyone was eager to stay in the Netherlands as long as possible. That was what I found so important about Westerbork, no matter how gruesome it was.

My contact with Otto Frank was very short, as were many contacts in Westerbork. Later, sadly, I saw the two girls again. People who were taken out of the punishment barracks were never seen again. It goes without saying that you never again saw the people who went on the transport. In the evenings, there was an announcement of the names of those who would have to go, and there was always the fear that your name might be included. You were always thinking, Oh, I hope the liberation will come soon. Because we did get news that the liberation was imminent. It was a race against time, and we all hoped for it. Sadly enough, that hope didn't materialize.

Several days before we went on the transport, a group of us—mainly political prisoners, people who had been in the resistance, were brought up, very officially, before the highest Nazi commanders Gemmeker, Aus der Fünten, and Fischer. There the accusations against us were read aloud, and then we could leave. I had already had a terrible feeling that something awful was about to happen. That was just before that last transport of September 3, 1944. In the evening, the names were read out. Mine was included. Yes, then you knew; you were leaving the Netherlands, and then you could simply give up all hope.

We were taken in cattle cars, in fits and starts, making many stops. It soon became clear to me that we were going to Poland.

It was very embarrassing in that car. People had to do their business openly. From time to time, there was a gentleman who would stand in front of you, which in itself was also embarrassing, but you were glad that you were hidden for a moment.

A giant of a man, a Pole named Loew, was with us. Because he was so tall, he could look out through the bars of the little window which was up high in the cattle car. He could tell approximately which way we were going. He became very excited when he recognized his home. And then we understood that we were in the vicinity of Auschwitz.

Upon our arrival in Auschwitz, so many things rushed at me that they were scarcely comprehensible, so that you lost your sense of good and evil. Our names were called out, and men, old men, children, young mothers with children were separated from us. We were taken to a little office, where there were women sitting in rows, and we had to bare our left arm and we were tattooed with numbers there. My number is 88410.

We had to open our mouths, because gold teeth and fillings

were registered. All things were so singularly and overwhelmingly humiliating. I felt just like an animal—you always look inside the mouth of an animal.

After that, there was the selection, which I only understood afterward. Long rows were formed. Mengele, I think, was standing there. I don't know this for sure—he didn't introduce himself. To the left, to the right. Mrs. van Schaik stood in front of me; she had to go to the left. I looked back at her, and I got a hard blow from the man who was selecting us and he asked me, "Do you want to go that way too?" And he pushed me to the right, because that's where I belonged, to the right. Fortunately Mrs. van Schaik was able to join us later. How, I don't know. She said that she had been through terrible situations.

Then we went to Birkenau, the women's camp, our destination. There I met Mrs. Kautsky, the widow of Karl Kautsky, the German social democratic leader, who had fled to the Netherlands in 1933 and had died there. But after a few days, I never saw her again. I naturally felt very attracted to this woman.

We were taken to barracks, yes, animal pens. We had to stay there the whole day—no work, absolutely nothing to do. The difficult thing for me and for many others was that you couldn't go outside when you had to go to the toilet. Awful. We were together with Polish, Czech, French, Belgian, and Hungarian women—a whole mishmash. We never saw a lot of the women who had been on the transport again. We didn't know whether they were in other barracks.

What was so dreadful, also in Birkenau, was that constant roll call. Each time, outside again, sometimes for entire Sundays, in the cold and rain. Often we were naked too, because you were examined: every scratch, every pimple, might mean death for you. The Polish women, who had faced this sort of selection process much longer than we, ducked it. But we Dutch women didn't know how to go about that. We stood for roll call very obediently. Where could we have gone? Imagine, if we had tried to duck it, we would have been grabbed right away. We didn't bother trying—we simply couldn't do it.

There was a very nice, red-haired woman, Julia, in our group, who came into conflict with Hanka. Hanka, a *Kapo* about sixteen or seventeen years old, was rather rough with us; she hit us with a stick. Again and again we had to line up, and God forbid if the numbers didn't tally, if one was missing, we were counted again, counted anew, unendingly. The counting was especially important when we were inspected for scratches and so forth, because then the numbers had to tally precisely. Then she had to enter the number of people she had counted on a list.

Julia couldn't stand it that Hanka treated us that way, and she rebelled. "Who do you think you are? When we get out of here, I'm going to marry one of the most important men in Holland." She survived the camp and later married the diamond merchant, Jo Asscher.

After Julia had confronted Hanka that way, Hanka told us that her parents had been killed on the very spot where she was standing—and she pointed to the place—beaten to death. And she continued, "I've been here for years, and you've just arrived."

I think that Hanka had a rather distorted image of Dutch people insofar as we, as Dutch Jews, had indeed led very protected lives; we could develop as we wanted to and learn what we wanted to if we had the opportunities. As a Polish Jew, she hadn't been able to do that. She saw a group of Dutch women there, well fed and healthy and not yet hungry. When she told us that, I understood her better. I forgave her behavior. I assume that she had no idea where the Netherlands were—a very distant land that she possibly had never heard of. And then a group of women arrived who hadn't yet gone through anything, and she didn't like that.

Next to us we saw a marked-off area with gypsy women and children who were yelling, screaming. The next day, they weren't there. We understood, but we didn't know exactly what was going on. We only saw that later.

We were taken several times to a large hall, where we had

96

to take our clothes off and be disinfected. That penetrating odor still pursues me from time to time. It is very special, the smell of that disinfectant.

And then we went to the sauna. That was the first time I heard that word, in a much different meaning than the current one, but I still can't stand hearing the word. We had to sit there, undressed, and then we would go to the infamous bath with the showers. That first time, I didn't know what that meant. Water came out; otherwise, I wouldn't be here to tell about it.

The second time, I saw through the bars—the Nazis used a lot of bars—girls screaming for dear life behind the bars. They were probably already in the positions where they would be gassed. And then we knew. We heard them, too. Finally you saw, all the time, the furnace with a huge flame. You smelled the scorched flesh. And everywhere, you saw the despair. It was a terrible, hopeless existence.

In the washroom, such as it was, sometimes with, sometimes without water, there were wash bowls lined up behind each other, and showers. I met Miss Leopold there. I had worked in the Bijenkorf store for thirteen years, from 1928 until my dismissal in 1941. I had gotten to know Miss Leopold there. She was a very elegant woman who always looked wonderful. She was the head of the art department. There was nothing left of her elegance, nothing. She was standing there, washing herself; she was thin and looked terrible.

I also met Bella Fierlier there. I'd like to say something more about her. Bella worked with me in the office at the Bijenkort like many other Jews. She was a simple, sweet, outgoing girl of sixteen. Now Bella had suddenly become an old woman with old knowing eyes. She had been there much longer than we had. I saw her every day and always talked to her. One day, Bella came up to me to say good-bye. "I've come to say good-bye to you. My number was listed today. I'm going to the furnaces."

Despite my being there, despite the fact that I knew by then what was going on in Birkenau, that was really the worst thing that happened to me. It was harrowing, it was tragic, it was terrible. I tried to console her. "Oh, Bella, how do you know that? Perhaps it will turn out all right. You can never know."

Then she said, "I know; tomorrow, I'm going to the furnaces."

That same child, that innocent, sweet, nice girl, spoke those words and, to this day, I have never been able to forget that.

The most awful executions and tortures took place in front of us at the large roll-call place. We were forced to face the misery. We saw the gallows, we saw carts with corpses, pulled by moving corpses, skeletons, with ropes over their shoulders, who moved the carts forward, while we heard the sound of the orchestra playing the song, "Rats, bread, and beans." After the war, I couldn't listen to that song anymore.

I especially remember Marcelle Wertheim-Citroen. She used her little ration of margarine, not to eat with the piece of bread that was given to us, but to smear onto her face. We all found this tragicomic. It didn't help Marcelle; we never saw her again.

I also had a lot of contact with Elly de Jong. She was was married to an artist, a mixed marriage. She came from a good family. Her father was the owner of a sugar plantation and she was brought up by a governess, which she really found very embarrassing, because she had socialist ideas. She told me a moving story. As a young woman, she once went to a fortune teller who asked her to give him something personal—an article of clothing. She didn't have anything readily at hand other than a glove. The fortune teller said, "No, I can't tell you; go away, right now. I can't tell you what I see." She relived this experience so clearly, and now she knew what he had seen. People reached back into their past for this kind of thing.

We heard rumors about the liberation, that the Russians were getting closer, and we all thought, If only I don't have to go to the gas chamber at the last minute. Planes flew overhead. I always looked at those airplanes. I thought, Why, why don't they bombard these camps? I realized that that would also mean the end for us, but nonetheless it seemed more honorable than to go to the gas ovens. It didn't happen. Why not? An open question.

The Allies must have known, after all; we understood that. And that they just let us go to hell, did nothing, and also let the trains go on running to Auschwitz, to Birkenau, continuously, even though they knew what was going on. Now we know that the war was much more important to them than the Jews. That probably answers the open question.

———

I always envied the birds who could fly away. It seemed so fantastic to me to be able to fly, to go wherever you wanted to, and you couldn't do that anymore in the camp. Birds were the leitmotiv in all the camps. You saw the birds everywhere; everywhere, there were birds, even in Auschwitz, even in Birkenau, and certainly in Bergen-Belsen, where it was so beautifully green and, at the same time, so gruesomely gray.

Hunger wasn't yet prevalent among us Dutch women in Auschwitz. We didn't get enough, but we had, after all, been well fed in Westerbork, where there was no hunger, because there were people, even in the punishment barracks, who got packages. I also got a package there once. You were fed, and what one didn't have, another did. There was a very good atmosphere of solidarity in the punishment barracks in Westerbork. In Auschwitz and Birkenau, I also didn't suffer much from hunger.

I did see skeletons there, people who had gradually become completely emaciated. They were in fact called *muzelmannen* (people who were clearly starving, who were literally skin and bones). But I never got a clear picture of how it could get so bad for them and why they didn't go into the gas chambers.

In Auschwitz, I never dwelled on the question of how to get out of there alive. I had become familiar with that constant smoking furnace and that flame. I didn't know anything. I didn't know why I had to stand for roll call, why I wasn't there, in that sea of flames. I have never understood how even one person came out of there alive.

I couldn't comprehend that people went into the gas chambers—that was too colossal. You absolutely had to shut yourself off from that, because at any moment it could happen to you, too. If they discovered anything about you, if, for example, you just weren't standing in the place where you belonged, then you wouldn't know whether your number would be listed or not. Actually, there no reason was needed for your name to be listed—look at Bella, look at Miss Leopold, whom I met daily. What had they done? So your chances were just as great. Her now, you next.

I really believe that that feeling of unreality was a part of my survival: to distance myself, distance myself from the situation, distance myself from eating. Because existence was so difficult, to stay on your feet, to be a bit human, the little that was necessary so that you could still have a conversation. But feelings of death—they are so difficult to describe, because when you saw those skeletons go by, yes, that was a spectacle so awful, you just couldn't let yourself get involved. That pity for others was pity for yourself, and I absolutely didn't want that. Because once you started, then you would gradually fall apart. And that was really my strength. I certainly didn't want to lose it. I didn't want to die, although I knew that there was a 100 percent chance that I would. That was exactly what was so crazy, that we didn't all go into the flames. I still wonder about that. Fortunately, I don't think about it every day, but there are indeed moments when I simply cannot understand it.

We were very happy to leave Auschwitz. We went on a transport to Bergen-Belsen. The Russians were in the vicinity and the Nazis wanted to get us away. It is, of course, still strange, if you seriously think it over. Why were we put on those transports again, when they surely had all the means to end our lives?

The group which went to Bergen-Belsen consisted of a lot

100

of women whom I had gotten to know in Birkenau, including a few whom I knew from Westerbork. Some of the women in our group stayed behind. New groups were being formed all the time. But few Dutch women went the same way as I did.

Suddenly before our departure, there was unrest in Auschwitz. There were rumors that the Russians were close by. Did that mean an accelerated complete extermination, everyone to the gas chambers? Or did it offer a little hope for some kind of liberation, although it was difficult to understand how that would take place? But extermination was, of course, the objective of Auschwitz and Birkenau. The gas chamber had to work and the furnaces had to burn.

We went on the transport. Initially, you were very happy— to be away from the horror—the chance that you could be gassed at any moment. Maybe a better chance, a better chance to live. We all got a chunk of bread, with a dab of margarine and a piece of goat cheese. Awful—as Dutch people, we had never had that, and we thought that it was really disgusting. There was a lively trade in goat cheese and garlic. The Polish women were crazy about garlic and were prepared to trade a slice of bread for a clove of garlic. We Dutch women didn't participate in that very much, because garlic was an unknown item to us in those years.

Every train trip—and this one as well—was accompanied by tension, fear, and terrible conditions. You didn't know how long it would last, you didn't know where you were going. They didn't tell you that, of course. It was cold, bitter cold, and it goes without saying that we weren't well dressed. And there was the uncertainty about how long it would last. Many people were packed close together in such trains, and there were many irritations. No one could hold out very long from doing their business, so there was a terrible stench. Everywhere, people were weeping. You were always crowded together; you never had a place. You sat for days on end in that freight car, and always a soldier at the entrance with his weapon. We slept once in a while, but most of the time it was out of the question.

Bergen-Belsen, where we finally arrived, looked very, very beautiful, because it was green and there were trees. Nature was beautiful there, certainly not all that bleakness of Auschwitz.

Bergen-Belsen had not planned for so many women. We went to a different camp from the one that had been in existence. Again, we were convicts, and we were put in a large tent that had been set up very carelessly. Hundreds and hundreds of women. But a severe storm tore down the tent and we were dragged along. The rain changed everything into a huge, cold sea of mud where we had to stand. Many of us got bladder inflammations and diarrhea. There was awful chaos.

We had no idea what was happening to us. We looked at each other—there were only a few Dutch women, but yes, I liked the others just as much. We were again together with many different sorts of women.

We stayed in that collapsed tent for several days. Meanwhile, they found shelter for us in the existing barracks. How that happened, I don't know—I didn't really pay attention. You were taken away again, and you were told nothing. You just went along. You weren't anything more than a kind of herd animal. We wound up in barracks and were assigned to bunks, two by two. Whether you knew each other, whether you liked each other, didn't matter. That's the way it had to be. Right away, you looked for a place. If there was a free place, you were very happy. It was important to get along with your bunk mate. Most of the time that worked out.

I was in the upper bunk with a girl named Margulies. In the evenings, she would go to the barbed-wire fence which wasn't so far from us. Behind that fence was the so-called free camp. She would come back with a bit of mustard. Up to that time I had no idea that it was so delicious, because I got a lick of mustard too; it was especially tasty. She went there every evening.

As far as possible, I controlled any genuine feeling of hunger. I heard women speaking, especially in our barracks in Bergen-

Belsen, about what they would all eat when they were free again. A fried egg, prepared in a variety of ways. Entire dinners were fantasized—I almost got sick from it and thought, Not that, I won't succumb to that.

Above all, my attention was focused on freedom. I wouldn't admit that one piece of bread more or less would be my salvation. And from the very beginning, since my arrest on the train, I had reckoned that this was the end. So every day that I was still alive was so much gained. Hunger pangs didn't do you any good. Not that I wasn't hungry, of course. We were all hungry. But I kept that image of freedom in front of me. I feared for my husband and children, and those feelings dominated me. That feeling of fear actually played the largest role in being a prisoner. What, after all, was a hard-earned piece of bread if you had to go to the barbed-wire fence to get it, and all sorts of things like that, to people you didn't even know? I simply let it go. I was also afraid of getting punished if I were caught, and furthermore, I wanted to save my strength.

I saw Anne and her sister Margot again in the barracks. Her parents weren't there. You didn't ask about that because you actually knew . . . given your own experience with parents, brothers, and so forth. Yes, you had a suspicion, but no more than that. The Frank girls were almost unrecognizable since their hair had been cut off. They were much balder than we were; how that could be, I don't know. And they were cold, just like all the rest of us.

It was winter and you didn't have any clothes. So all of the ingredients for illness were present. They were in bad shape. Day by day they got weaker. Nevertheless, they went to the fence of the so-called free camp every day, in the hope of getting something. They were very determined. I'm virtually certain that they met someone there whom they knew. They took a large risk, because it was forbidden and our *Kapos* weren't lenient. Sometimes they got a package which had been thrown over to them. Then they would come back elated, very happy, and they would sit down and eat what they had gotten

103

with great pleasure. But you could see that they were very sick.

The Frank girls were so emaciated. They looked terrible. They had little squabbles, caused by their illness, because it was clear that they had typhus. You could tell even if you had never had anything to deal to do with that before. Typhus was the hallmark of Bergen-Belsen. They had those hollowed-out faces, skin over bone. They were terribly cold. They had the least desirable places in the barracks, below, near the door, which was constantly opened and closed. You heard them constantly screaming, "Close the door, close the door," and the voices became weaker every day.

You could really see both of them dying, as well as others. But what was so sad, of course, was that these children were still so young. I always found it so horrible that as children, they had never really lived. They were indeed the youngest among us. The rest of us were all a bit older.

They showed the recognizable symptoms of typhus—that gradual wasting away, a sort of apathy, with occasional revivals, until they became so sick that there wasn't any hope. And their end came. I don't know which one was carried out earlier, Anne or Margot. Suddenly, I didn't see them anymore, so I had to assume that they had died. Look, I didn't pay any special attention to them because there were so many others who also died. When I didn't see them again, I assumed that they had died there, down there on that bunk. One fine day, they weren't there any longer—actually, a bad day.

The dead were always carried outside, laid down in front of the barracks, and when you were let out in the morning to go to the latrine, you had to walk past them. That was just as dreadful as going to the latrine itself, because gradually everyone got typhus. In front of the barracks was a kind of wheelbarrow in which you could take care of your needs. Sometimes you also had to take those wheelbarrows to the latrine. Possibly it was on one of those trips to the latrine that I walked past the bodies of the Frank sisters, one or both—I don't know. At the time, I assumed that the bodies of the Frank girls had also been put down in front of the barracks. And then the heaps would be cleared away. A huge hole would be dug and they were thrown into it. That I'm sure of. That must have been their fate, because that's what happened with other people. I don't have a single reason for assuming that it was any differ- ent for them than for the other women with us who died at the same time.

Then I got a notice that a Mrs. Van Amerongen was looking for someone whose name was also Van Amerongen. The situa- tion was that the diamond merchants in the so-called free camp were going on a transport, and their wives and children were no longer protected. I went there and found my mother- in-law. From that time on I went there every day until I was forbidden to do so because I was missed at roll call. They told me that I couldn't do it anymore because it endangered the others. So I didn't go there anymore until I learned that my mother-in-law had died. Then I went once again, and one of the Brilleslijper sisters, who nursed the people in that barracks, gave me my mother-in-law's coat and her wedding ring. These have remained precious to me—more precious than the most beautiful diamond jewelry.

I saw the Brilleslijper sisters daily and greatly admired the way they took care of the sick people and the elderly, closing their eyes when they died—my mother-in-law as well. I ad- mired that very much.

I, too, got sick—we were all sick—I also had typhus. I lay there in the lower bunk because I couldn't make it to the top bunk. I heard our doctor, Dr. Knorringa-Boekdrukker, off in the distance, saying, when he was asked to give me an aspirin, "Well, actually not; she won't make it through the evening." Whether this was a stimulus for me, I don't know. The fact is that I recovered and Dr. Knorringa died.

Dying was the order of the day in Bergen-Belsen. Probably fewer people died there than in Birkenau, but it was more visible. In Birkenau, entire groups would simply disappear— the entire gypsy camp disappeared. There wasn't even any mourning. Whether you were skinny or not skinny, sick or not sick, you vanished. In Birkenau; if your name was listed, you were gone. As far as that goes, it was efficient and neat. In Bergen-Belsen, you didn't say good-bye, you died slowly, from illness, exhaustion, cold, most of them from hunger. Most of the people were apathetic. Typhus makes you apathetic. It affects your brain.

But you don't learn to live with death. I remember when I went to see my mother-in-law that I fell over bodies because it was dark. You had to go early in the morning, before the roll call. Although you often fell over dead bodies, every time it happened it was again a shock. I couldn't get used to it.

The period in Bergen-Belsen was certainly the most wretched. You knew so little about how the war was going; you didn't know how long it would last, and because of the illness, you became convinced that death was lying in wait. Let me put it this way: In Birkenau you were young and still looked fine. You couldn't be thin, you couldn't be a skeleton, you couldn't have a pimple, you surely couldn't have any sores or boils. You had to be flawless. As long as you were, you had a chance, until you weren't. We were transported before it got that far.

But in Bergen-Belsen, death lay in wait on all sides. You saw death, you noticed it so much more than in Birkenau, where the people who were going downhill simply disappeared. Whoever remained was apparently healthy. In Bergen-Belsen, you stared death in the face at every moment. For others, for yourself. You got weaker. Especially when I got typhus, I would think, This is it; this is the end. I felt that very clearly. It is an inexplicable miracle that I made it.

There is no medical explanation for this. Especially after Dr. Knorringa thought that I wouldn't make it through that night. That is actually the greatest miracle, but I don't know what did it: will power, spiritual strength, the will to see husband and child again. I don't know; I don't have a logical explanation for it.

I myself was also apathetic, despite my will power. On the one hand, there was the will to survive; on the other hand, there was the apathy—this can't be done, this is impossible, how can you get out, what means will get you out, out of this horrible situation. I never expected to be liberated by the Allies. You stayed alive, but don't ask how, sick and powerless, with so many dead around you. I still find it miraculous that a few other people from this barracks survived.

Then, one day, we had to stand for roll call again, on the large roll-call place. People with years of camp experience tried to hide. They were panic-stricken about a transport. But I wasn't. I thought only of getting out of this hell, having a chance to get out. I also didn't know how to make myself inconspicuous; that required a certain kind of skill, which we Dutch people still hadn't mastered.

Three Germans came to the roll-call place, out of uniform. That was remarkable, it was encouraging. You had a glimpse of the outside world again. It seemed that those three men were looking for female slave laborers. A large number of women went again on the transport, but I don't know where they went.

Soon we found out that we were going, in cattle cars again, to Raguhn. Raguhn is a very small place near Halle, in the vicinity of Leipzig. There was an airplane factory there, where people who weren't prisoners also worked, and prisoners filled in for the missing labor force. According to official data, we arrived there on February 12, 1945.

I was selected, along with nine Polish women, to peel potatos in a potato cellar. Of course, that was heaven on earth. It was much better than any other camp. We were in clean barracks, there was a place to wash, we got a blanket. But was this another trick, or was it really as nice as it seemed? It was just as nice as it looked, as long as you could peel potatoes, as long as you worked and ate that good potato soup, and it wasn't forbidden to eat a small potato once in a while. So we were in a relatively good situation.

The three German women who worked there, who boiled and prepared the potatoes, didn't understand anything. They had been told that a transport would come, with convicts who had crimes on their consciences. Yet here were ten women, who worked, who were obedient, who were respectable. But they couldn't talk to us because there was a *Kapo* there, a Dutch woman from 's-Hertogenbosch, who did her work well. We were only allowed to talk to each other about the work, and not with those German women. But we did, very secretively. They were very nice to us—they didn't understand any of it. You mustn't imagine that Raguhn was like Berlin or another large German city. It was a small hamlet, where two Jews lived—they were still living there, married to non-Jews. I have to assume that they really didn't know what was happening to the Jews. At Easter, we got a piece of cake from them. That was something so human, wasn't it? Especially the gesture itself. You felt a little more like a human being.

Every day, led by that Dutch *Kapo* from 's-Hertogenbosch, we went from the barracks to the kitchen through the only street of Raguhn, she and we ten women.

The other women were eager for us to bring them potatoes. It was dangerous. I did it, was caught, and was punished. What I had to do was to draw water from a brook that had steep banks, because they wanted to blow up a bridge in case the enemy got closer, and they needed water for the dynamite. I could hardly endure it, but I had to do it. The gentle commandant was walking around—it was just a small place—and asked me why I wasn't working in the kitchen any longer.

I told him and said, "Look, my fellow prisoners are hungrier than I am. It seems logical to me that I should give them some of the potatoes."

Then he said, "Very well, starting tomorrow, you can go back to the kitchen. But don't do it again."

Then this too came to an end, and we went on transport again. That was an awful transport, because we were on the verge of being liberated and they were trying to prevent it.

108

Orders arrived from the women's camp that was under the jurisdiction of Ravensbrück, saying that we had to leave. No one knew where we were going. It was a terrible transport because many of the people could no longer manage to get out of the cattle cars every time to relieve themselves.

Even worse, there were women who didn't have the strength to climb back into the cars. They stayed behind and were irretrievably lost.

There wasn't any more food. That situation lasted for days. No one knew where we were going, and I think the train engineer didn't either.

Ebbe, a very small woman, was on that trip. She spoke only Italian and had made a very naive impression. When the train stopped, to our complete amazement she disappeared and never came back, perhaps she escaped.

Finally, they probably heard that Theresienstadt hadn't been liberated yet, and that's where we landed and were liberated later.

I was able to share in a lovely moment there in Theresienstadt, walking alone with a girlfriend, free, able to think calmly. After a few days, a coal truck came, with Americans. Three women of whom I was one, left with them. First we came to Bamberg. There was another camp there where you had to report, and then we went on a Rhine barge back to Holland, to freedom.

I learned later that sixteen women in our group, some of whom were already exhausted when they arrived in Raguhn, had died there. Twelve of them are buried in the cemetery there. Four of them were reburied in their homeland, including Betty Labzowski from Zierikzee. She died, at the age of twenty-five, and was reburied in the Netherlands.

Maybe I was able to survive because I had had a bit more knowledge of life, a bit more will to live as well. I am assuming that, because I have it to this day. Every day I can still enjoy life—which sounds strange—but that's how it is. I try to make a celebration of every day of my life. That's not always successful, but I try to do it. I think that that was a decisive factor, that particular spiritual strength. My daughter always says, "Mama is a rock."

In Israel, where we live, Anne Frank is a legend, and at the same time, a living girl. People are very interested in her. I believe that there is an Anne Frank Street in practically every town. Her diary has been translated into modern Hebrew.

People think that she is very special. Once, when my daughter was in the Netherlands with her twin daughters, one of the first things they wanted me to show them was the Anne Frank House. I didn't feel up to it; actually, I didn't want to go at all. For more than forty years, I had pushed that aside because I really wanted to live normally, and I didn't want to talk about it anymore.

Nonetheless, I went to the Anne Frank House, and I had a very special feeling there. I had seen her, after all, from the time that she came to Westerbork. People took pictures there of every corner, every plank, everything; especially the Japanese, who you would suppose wouldn't be as emotionally touched as the Europeans. My daughter panicked, because she knew that I had known Anne. She looked around and she said, "Mama, shouldn't you tell these people that you knew her? Shouldn't you do something? Tell them, tell them."

I couldn't do it; I absolutely couldn't. I wouldn't have known how to tell it. Because it was so bizarre, that entire Anne Frank House. All those people, all those cameras. I saw Anne again and I thought that this really wouldn't have been anything for her. In the Anne Frank House, you can see what I wrote in the registration book: "Anne Frank didn't want this."

Rachel van Amerongen–Frankfoorder has added the following dedication:
In memory of Charles Desiré Lu-A-Si, who fought from the very first hour and was killed in 1942 by the Nazis.

BLOEME
EVERS-EMDEN

Willy Lindwer

Bloeme Evers-Emden.

Bloeme Evers is a small, valiant, and special woman. She occupies a prominent position in the Jewish women's organization, Deborah and is active in the Jewish-Religious life of Amsterdam. She is inseparable from her husband, Hans, who is also active in Amsterdam Jewish life. Each meeting with Bloeme is a special experience.

In one of the first conversations I had with Bloeme, she said she could remember only a few of the details from the period when she was in the concentration camps. However, she was able to uniquely articulate her feelings and to analyze the depth of the mortifications that she endured as an eighteen-year-old girl. When she took her final high school examination in 1943, she was the only student left in the class; her classmates had all been arrested or had gone into hiding. She thought it unlikely that her diploma would ever be of any use to her.

Many years after the war, Bloeme completed her studies in psychology at the university, despite the responsibilities of a large family. Recently, she completed her thesis and is now a doctor of psychology.

Bloeme got to know Anne and Margot Frank in the Jewish Lyceum. In 1941, this preparatory school was designated for Jewish children. In Auschwitz-Birkenau Bloeme formed a strong friendship with Lenie de Jong–van Naarden and a number of other women that helped them survive an unbearable time. Of this group, five died. Their remembrance is a blessing to those who survived.

The names of the eight women who were together in the concentration camps for nine months and who shared love and sorrow were: Nettie, Lydia, Lenie, Annie, Rosy, Rootje, Anita, and Bloeme. They had a very special relationship that continues still.

113

Bloeme Evers-Emden

To say now that I was "born in sunshine with a sigh from the raging sea," no, that isn't true. I came from an Amsterdam working class background. I was born in 1926. My father was a diamond cutter and my mother was a seamstress. I had a good, though poor, youth, in which political conversations and political consciousness were of central concern. My father was convinced that the world could be improved; when poverty was abolished, all people would be good. The same thing was emphasized by the many people who came to visit us. They debated with one another, particularly about what had been happening with the Jews in Germany since 1933. Next to the warm protection of the family, this shaped my youth.

We were part of a large family and a large circle of acquaintances. Although my parents had renounced religion, the surroundings in which I grew up were truly Jewish.

When the war broke out in 1940, we understood that the persecution of Jews would not be restricted to German Jews.

My father showed his political insight; in 1942, he said, "We will go under, but so will Germany."

Nevertheless, he made no effort to escape. He didn't dare to go into hiding. My mother wanted to, but nothing came of it. My father made a heroic effort to save me from deportation. That was the end of 1942. Then I got a summons, and in his despair, he went to the Euterpestraat, where the *Zentralstelle für Jüdische Auswanderung* (Central Authority for Jewish Emigration) had been set up. He went all the way to Aus der Fünten himself (the SS director of the Jewish Emigration office), not knowing that he was such a high official. He was able to get my summons canceled and to arrange temporary exemption from deportation for me. Nothing less than a miracle! That worked until 1943 and then it was over.

In 1941 the measures against Jewish schoolchildren began. First, the Jewish teachers were fired. In 1941 Jewish children had to leave the public schools to go to a newly established school, the Jewish Lyceum. We were transferred to a school building on the Mauritskade. Later, we moved to the Stadstimmertuinen, across from the real Jewish high school.

At that time, I met Margot and Anne. Margot was in another class, at the same level as mine. I had contact with her, but we weren't friends. And I did know Anne, but when you were in High School you didn't have much to do with such a young child, in a lower class.

They gave the impression that they were very well-bred, with good manners—a gain for the school. Not that I realized that then, but in looking back, I see it that way.

As a result of my father's intervention I remained safe until 1943. The classes shrank. When you went to school on Mondays there would once again be children absent, and you just hoped that they were sick. But most of the time it turned out that either they had been taken away, or, they had gone into hiding. Nobody was up to concocting the usual schoolchild pranks; there was an atmosphere of hard work. Certainly because of the pressure of what was happening in the world, but also because for a short time we still had the privilege of pursuing our education.

In 1943, I was in the fifth class—the class in which you take the final examinations. At the end of April or the beginning of May, the written exams started. There were three of us left: two boys—Meijer de Hond and Siegfried Natkiel—and I. In the period that we were free before the final oral examinations, they disappeared too. I have never learned anything more about Meijer. Siegfried went into hiding, was arrested, escaped from Westerbork, and I know that he is still alive.

Thus, I took the final oral exams as the only remaining student. All the members of the examination committee were there—quite strange for this one young girl, not even seventeen years old. The oral exams took place on Monday and Tuesday, four tests in the morning and two in the afternoon. You took final exams in twelve subjects.

After the Monday morning session, my friend came to get me and said, "They were at your house this morning; you're going to be picked up this evening." Just then there was an air raid warning, and we had to seek shelter. I went into the school with my friend. Probably because of this coincidence, I considered whether it might be possible to complete all the exam subjects that day. I went to the director, explained the situation, and he was able to get together all the committee members and the teachers who had to attend the exams. And I finished those final exams. The teachers' meeting was very short. I was called in to get my diploma. It was a terrible scene. I went home with my diploma, and I thought that it was very unlikely that it would ever do me any good. I understood that very well.

I was indeed picked up that evening and transported to the Hollandse Schouwburg (Dutch Theater), where I had been a number of times. My mother had stressed a few things that I took to heart: "Try not to be registered and find a family which can be like parents to you." And I did both. I had a backpack and another purse with me and by setting the purse down here, picking up the backpack and setting it down there and then bringing the purse here and again setting it down, I was able to pass the registration tables without being registered. And I did indeed link up with a fairly young family, who were willing to take me in temporarily as their daughter.

A cousin of mine had a friend who worked in the theater. I knew that friend. I told him that I had been successful in avoiding registration and that I wanted to get out. He said he would try to arrange it. I asked him every day if plans had been worked out yet, and on the third or fourth day, they were ready. I had a hiding place with friends of my parents.

Now, I had kicked off the back part of one of my shoes when I had entered the theater, and just that morning there was an announcement that whoever had something for the shoemaker could bring it and it would be repaired and brought back on the same day. So I took that shoe in, and walked with a sock on one foot and a shoe on the other. That very day, my cousin's friend came to say, "Listen, when the young children gather in the hall this evening to go to the nursery, go and stand there, and you can cross with them." The nursery was across the street from the Hollandse Schouwburg.

"I only have one shoe," I said.

"Yes," he said, "wait and see; perhaps the it'll be back in time."

But it wasn't, and I told my adopted "parents" about my plan and asked them to have my shoe brought to the other side of the street. The bell rang—the signal that the children had to say good-bye to their parents because they were going to the nursery. That farewell was indescribable, because no one knew whether they would see their children the next day. But I had made no allowance for that, so that when the bell rang and I went to the hall, there wasn't a child to be seen with whom I could cross the street. But to go back would have been very conspicuous too since an SS man was guarding the entrance. I stood there, dreadfully nervous and undecided. Then the SS

117

man turned around and snarled, *"Was machen Sie dort* (What are you doing there)?" I froze on the spot, unable to give him an answer. I saw how he looked me over and how he stared at that one shoeless foot. He shrugged his shoulders and turned around.

Shortly thereafter the children finally came. I grabbed a few of their hands and crossed the street. In the course of the evening, my other shoe was indeed delivered.

The next morning, I was sent out to the street very early. I covered up my star (the Star of David which the Nazis required Jews to wear) and walked to Nieuw-West, at the edge of the city. It was a three-hour walk, I think. But no one was at home at the address where I was to go into hiding—not for the entire day; they were at work. I had an aunt and an uncle who lived there in the neighborhood who were able to tell my parents. They came. That was the last time that I saw my parents.

That evening, I went back to the house where I went into hiding, to Truus and Floor de Groen. After all these years, I still have a warm relationship with Truus. Their house was a center of underground activities and they really didn't want to have an *onderduiker* there because it put them into a great deal of danger. They said, "If there is a raid, you'll be right there; we can't have any *onderduikers.*" Still, it took about six weeks before they found another address for me.

That was the beginning of a real ordeal. I remember very well that I didn't allow feelings to enter my consciousness. I was literally pursued—here for a week, there for an afternoon—fifteen addresses in three months. Finally, I landed in a nursing home where I was taken on as a nursing assistant. The woman who was the director knew what was going on. I worked there for nine months. Then there was a raid—it seems that there were Jewish patients there. They were taken away. Apparently they weren't looking for me, but for security reasons, I had to leave the next morning. First I had to go to the office to pick up my false papers. They were given to me by the young woman in there, and I will never forget that two tears glistened in her eyes.

After a long period of wandering, I was hired as a servant in Rotterdam. On the advice of the *onderduik* organization, to which I belonged, I didn't tell them that I was Jewish. I don't know what the organization people were thinking, but I did take their advice. I spent a couple of pleasant months with a very nice woman and her son. I think that I was a hard-working maid. In the beginning, I wasn't so handy, but I had already learned a lot in the nursing home.

After a certain time, the people went on vacation, and I wondered, Where can I stay? The *onderduik* organization advised, "Come here for those fourteen days," and during those two weeks, the Nazis disbanded the organization. I would like to give the names of the people who worked there: Aad Zeegers and his sister, Mary ten Have-Zeegers. Later, Aad was shot. He was a great man.

Looking back, I know that period in hiding was only a prelude to something much worse, but so long as you didn't know anything else, being in hiding was very traumatic. People haven't paid enough attention to that. But it meant a loss of identity, occupation, your own context, your family, social networks, books, possessions. Everything was gone. In almost all cases, you had to subordinate yourself to good—and not so good—people. The loss of significant work from one day to the next, and on top of that, the fact that everything was better than the fate that the Germans had up their sleeves for you. All in all, it was a great trauma that could last for years. You could adjust to it, but the fact remains that its significance has not been fully considered.

I was in hiding for a total of fifteen months, from May 1943 to August 1944. After two weeks in the Haagse Veer, the prison in Rotterdam, the transport to Westerbork awaited me.

I went out of the frying pan into the fire.

In Westerbork, the first family I met was the Frank family

whom I had known from school. We exchanged stories of some of our experiences of being in hiding. Afterward, we saw each other regularly. I think—although I don't know it for certain any more—that I saw Margot at the tables where we worked on the batteries. We all wore the same overalls. Especially when we worked on the batteries; that was such filthy work.

One of the camp mates whom I remember well from the later period in Westerbork is Nettie. She became my camp mother; she was twenty years older. She and her husband, were like parents to me, roles which fit their character. For example, she dished out the food. When Nettie saw me for the first time, I probably made a somewhat forlorn impression, because she was very cordial. She said, "Come over here, child."

As far as Lenie goes, I first met her naked at the faucet. We stood across from each other in what was called the *Waschraum* (washroom). That consisted of oblong zinc troughs. Here and there, the water splashed down from the faucets. I had already met Rosy and Rootje in the Haagse Veer, but our group of friends only formed gradually in Auschwitz.

I can't tell much more about Westerbork. I do remember that you could manage if you adapted yourself to the circumstances. The work day was eight or nine or ten hours long. You wore overalls, because you were a criminal case, since you had been in hiding. (Later it turned out it wasn't significant at all, whether you were a criminal case or not.) There was also free time—there was a cabaret, and there was laughter. Only those transports were terrible—over and over again. Usually on Tuesdays. On Mondays, they called the names of the people who had to go.

I had indeed heard of extermination camps. But it was impossible to comprehend; you shut yourself off. No, you simply had to wait; the Nazis had you in their clutches. You didn't have any say in your fate or about your future. And the very worst could happen—you didn't want to know.

I can only remember a few things about those countless hours on that train from Westerbork to Auschwitz. I remember we were pressed against one another, not having any room and falling down in sleep—nothing more.

I do remember the arrival very well. The doors of the cars finally opened and men stood there in blue and white striped outfits. They screamed and kicked us out of the cars. I also remember suddenly seeing a woman talking to one of those people; I concluded that he was someone she knew and then I understood that they were prisoners as well.

We were taken, with our baggage, to a large area that was lit up by extraordinarily strong lights—so strong that I had the feeling that they were moons. I thought, We're on another planet—that crazy idea fit right into my experience. I think that that trip had somewhat dulled our awareness, allowing for thoughts that did not arise from ordinary reality. I thought, We have arrived on another planet after that trip, and here there are three moons.

The place was muddy. Some people stamped their valuables into the ground.

Then we were taken to rooms where we had to undress. That was an enormous shock for me. I was eighteen, shy, and had been brought up chastely, according to the prevailing morality. It goes without saying that I was embarrassed and ashamed. I remember an audible crack in my head, from being totally naked before the eyes of men. And then the thought came like a flash that, from then on, other norms and values would be in effect, that I would have to adjust to that, and that an entirely new life was beginning, or death was waiting.

The most horrible things happened to you as well as to others. Later, from reading Bruno Bettelheim's work, I learned about the strange experiences, protective mechanisms, called "derealization" and "depersonalization." Derealization is when reality is not experienced as reality: this cannot be true; this doesn't exist. And depersonalization, that is the phenomenon of a split of the personality: I stood to the side—and saw myself simultaneously walk on; object and subject at the same time. You are the object of your own observation, and at the

121

same time, you are the subject who walks off, or who is hungry, or who is suffering.

I also remember very well that I assimilated extremely sharp images and simultaneously shut off my feelings. I saw things with my eyes, but no more. Otherwise, you couldn't have survived, you couldn't have gotten through it.

From Auschwitz, I also remember that dull, terrible amazement that flooded over me when I learned that there were, apparently, people who were instructed to destroy other people, to kill, to annoy, to torment them to death. This was something that absolutely didn't fit into my image of humanity and the world, and I was stunned. I had heard and read stories. I could remember the events of 1941 in the Jewish neighborhood in Amsterdam, but you could still think of that as an excess or coincidence—a row that got out of hand, or whatever. But it turned out to be a system, not something that happened by chance.

I became very depressed knowing that such things existed. I didn't want to accept it. I had been brought up with respect for all people, insofar as they earned it on the basis of personal achievement or conduct, but not on the basis of race or heritage. I saw that the philosophy behind this system was carried out under the banner of a kind of inequality—an inferiority opposed to a superiority—and that the inferiors had to be crushed, whatever it took. To know this, and to be penetrated by this reality, was shattering.

Moreover, there was, of course, a huge difference between having heard and read about something, and experiencing it as reality, feeling also so powerless, like a bit of fluff in the wind. It was a long time before I got any grasp of this reality. That is, in the sense of being successful in adapting to the conditions and being able to give and receive support, and in that way exercise some influence.

In their treatment of people the goal of the SS was, aside from physical annihilation, to degrade a person, to take away completely—to really completely tear to pieces—to *destroy,* your self-respect, to make you into a rag, without any will. Because of the isolation, you were uncertain about everything. You didn't know how things stood with the war, you didn't know how it was progressing, you didn't know anything about the outside world, but you also didn't know anything about the "inside" world. You didn't know what you would do the next day, what they were up to—whether the doors of the gas chamber would open for you the next day. That was all a closed book. Something like that is real torment.

When someone is sick and doesn't know what disease he has, it is very frightening. But when a diagnosis is made, even if the diagnosis is bad news, you feel relief because you realize what you're up against. Now we never knew what we were up against.

The goal of the Germans was the disorganization, the disintegration of your personality. That didn't work with us, above all because of the mutual support that the members of our group of women gave each other, and because of what we had brought with us in terms of inner strength. In retrospect, I think that it is really quite marvelous to be able to establish that that is what made the difference.

After our arrival in Auschwitz, we landed in a bed for ten people. I don't remember very well how that worked out, but at a given moment, after several changes—Anita came there only later—this group was lying in that single bed. We joined together and drew consolation from crouching together on that bed and from the stories that we told each other during the many empty hours.

There was a lot of talk about food. But everyone also told her life story, her background, her feelings, and what it was like to be in hiding.

Our mutual bond as "sisters" and "mothers" was strengthened by the respect we bore for each other and the courtesy we showed each other. One of the things we did was to jointly keep up with the calendar. That was important too. Each day, we would say, for example, "Today is the twenty-first of De-

123

cember, 1944, Wednesday," out loud so that we wouldn't make a mistake.

As far as possible, the younger ones did things that were difficult for the older ones. Particularly, Lydia and Nettie, who were both twenty years older than I was, and whose strength gave way before mine did. I fetched water for them to wash themselves and did other things for them.

That strengthened the group, and I have the feeling that, the worse it got "outside," the better it became "inside." The German ideology didn't have a hold on us, not even for one second. Although they tried to drive home the idea of how worthless we were, just *blöde Kühe* (stupid cows), we never felt we were *Untermenschen* (subhumans).

But they did have a grip on our bodies. They could send us all over the place. They could do with us what they wanted, and they did. The senseless work that we sometimes had to do—for example, moving a pile of stones to the left and then back to the right—that was an attack on your dignity. I also remember feelings of intense shock, fear, and despair, but the group was there—the group that literally and figuratively kept each other on their feet.

It was a very consoling fact, to know that you could be yourself within that group—no matter what happened. We helped each other as much as possible. We didn't use any foul language, we upheld a high moral standard among ourselves, and we consoled each other.

I still remember the amazement I felt as I listened to my own words when it was, in a manner of speaking, my turn to say some words of courage: "Oh, you'll see, we're going to be freed, you'll see, it will happen." The next day someone else would say something uplifting, when I was prey to despair.

By the end of October, we had left Auschwitz and ended up in an *Arbeitslager* (work camp) in a small town, Libau, in Upper Silesia.

It doesn't happen to me often, but I had a prophetic dream there. In November, I said, "We will be liberated on the first sunny day in May." Naturally that was something everybody was eager to hear—I, myself, too.

The next day, I was depressed again and one of the women in the group said, "Bloeme, I listened very carefully to what you said yesterday. It's really true. You'll see, we will survive. We have to be very strong and help each other. Then we will live to see the liberation."

Our group, which, in the end, consisted of eight women, also found support in Ronnie van Cleef's group. Ronnie is a poet. During the time that she was in the camp, she wrote songs using opera and operetta melodies and practiced them with several women. On Sunday afternoons, during the free hours, they sang them and we sang along. That was an unimaginable source of strength—what a spiritual power. I have always been very thankful for that.

I also remember the very long night work at Libau—we had only one fifteen-minute break. I still see before me that very dimly lit factory hall where we gathered to eat soup. A small, dark Hungarian woman stood up and sang a well-known song in a crystal-clear voice. That was a thing of beauty from another world. A fragment of something esthetic which you had already completely forgotten existed.

I remember that once I was standing at roll call without any hope. Lenie stood behind me. She nudged me when the SS man wasn't looking for a moment, and said, "Do you see those mountains there—those snow-capped mountains? When we are liberated, we are going to dust them off." The power to say something like that kept you on your feet. These things were of immense significance.

My camp mother, Lydia, was an Orthodox Jew. Every day, she said her prayers. I had been brought up without any religion, but when I saw her mumbling, I knew that I couldn't disturb her. She was the first person who explained something to me about Jewishness.

As I said, we succeeded, despite the horrible circumstances, in keeping a high moral standard. To a great extent, that made it possible to prevent disintegration; that as well as the fact that it didn't last longer than three-fourths of a year.

I've read a lot about people who did disintegrate, people whose personalities changed because of their experiences in the camp. However, that didn't happen among us. I went in and came out again with the same character. Virtues and vices were perhaps intensified, but whoever was proud when she entered the camps, left them proud, in a manner of speaking. Whoever had a warm heart, had every opportunity to develop it further.

The attempts to degrade us to just a number completely failed in our group, as I see it. Had I become a number just because I had a number on my arm? Not for a minute. Our identity was not affected. I remained Bloeme Emden.

I can tell you something else. While we were in hiding, we used other names. You had to imprint yourself with those other names so that no matter what happened you wouldn't say your own name. But the alias was nothing more than a pasted-on label. However terrible it was to be arrested and deported, one thing was nice, and that was being able to use your own name again. Your name is so interwoven with your identity, your being, your existence—you can taste it, as it were, on your lips. To say your own name out loud: "I am Bloeme Emden." That felt good. And you don't get that from a number. Do you think you were addressed by your number in the group? What was my number . . . A.25106. "Hey, A.25106, rub my hands, please. I'm so cold."

The SS imposed a different kind of behavior on us, different norms and values, which you had to conform to outwardly as much as possible in order to, perhaps, survive, but it didn't penetrate to the core of your personality. You didn't internalize it. You were deeply convinced, and no one had to tell you, that their values were invalid and their norms were not norms at all. That what you had brought with you was inviolable. Your set of values, your conduct, what you deemed to be good and what you found to be evil—you brought that with you from your

126

upbringing, from your environment, and from everything that contributed to that.

They seemed like very badly programmed robots, those SS men. You had to do what they said, but that didn't mean that you accepted their values. I read that it did happen when people had been in the camps a long long time. But for us that was out of the question. When they verbally abused us, I remember that I was indifferent to it, I shed it like water off a duck's back. It didn't get to me, it slid over me, it had no meaning for my self-respect, my feelings toward myself or toward my friends or other people in the camp.

We didn't develop slave mentality either. I can give an example of this. When we were still working in the factory and the Russians were advancing, the supply of material for the tire chains we made became increasingly irregular. One day, a load did arrive. The woman who sat across from me at the assembly table said, *"Gott sei Dank—material* (Thank God, material)."

I considered her to have a slave mentality since she was thinking the thoughts of her "masters." Although I was only eighteen then, I haven't changed my opinion about this: someone with a slave mentality identifies with the oppressor.

Now it isn't true that you're not influenced by experiences. I think that a distinction has to be made between what the SS did and what the effects of it were. I've already mentioned my sad shock at finding that people had been trained to torment other people. I read that people sometimes identified with the SS. That didn't happen at all in our group. That's probably due to the fact that we, as a group, stayed in the background and didn't stand out from the anonymous, gray mass. Therefore we could more easily remain ourselves. For a short time, Lydia was a *Stubenälteste* (senior barracks leader), but that didn't affect her at all. She was the only one of us who was pushed to the forefront for a while.

Naturally, you couldn't get away from what was happening, but, together, you could erect an inner structure—with the group—so that it affected you as little as possible.

127

Still, the events that broke over us were so massive that many people thought it was a natural catastrophe for which the SS couldn't be held accountable; that the system wasn't the work of man. But I saw the distinction clearly; I said, "Yes, but the SS people are doing it."

After the war, I had an unfathomably deep contempt for everything that was German. I don't know how much of it was mingled with fear. My contempt was so deep that after the war was over, I didn't take anything from the German houses. Many of my fellow camp inmates went into the village and took what they needed. I don't condemn that, but I couldn't do it. I myself didn't even go to the village. It made me sick; to me, it was completely contaminated.

Many years after the war, we received some kind of payment—I actually don't remember anymore what it was—an indemnification for furniture or something like that. It was paid by check. I picked up that check at the post office and I held it by its corner. The post office was next to the bank where I took the check. There, holding it by that corner, I deposited it and I told them which Jewish institution should get the money. I don't want any money to remind me of what happened there. I have an intense aversion, a fathomless horror of that. I don't want to have anything more to do with it. I will never travel to Germany—never—or to Austria. Those are my special traumas.

Fortunately, I can usually handle the traumas I have left from the war reasonably well. And if I look back on it now, I think that there we had a tremendous internal self-defense against everything that happened to us, and that this saved our lives. But when that defense was no longer absolutely necessary, sometimes only many years after the war, it turned out that you were traumatized after all, and that you transmitted that to some degree to your children—certainly to those of your children who were receptive.

I still shut myself off from everything about war, from everything that deals with it, that there is to be read or seen. If

I don't, then I know that I will be sick again for a week from grief and misery. Assimilating the grief for lost family and for shattered social relationships—that has taken me decades.

In vitally important moments, that weighs very heavily. That makes you quite a bit more vulnerable. I think that the older you get, the more this shows itself. Without this part of your life history, you would certainly be much stronger. But in many respects I have an optimistic nature. Above all, I like to see, if possible, the the good side of everything.

I especially remember the last time I saw the Frank family. Another selection had taken place. I spoke to Mrs. Frank, who was with Margot. Anne was somewhere else; she had *Krätze* (scabies). She had a rash of some kind or other. The Germans, unhindered by medical knowledge—at least the Germans who had the say-so over our lives—were terribly afraid because it might be infectious and she had to be isolated. As a result, Anne couldn't go with our group. Mrs. Frank, echoed by Margot, said, "We are, of course, going with her." I remember that I nodded, that I understood that.

That was the last time I saw them.

Before that, we naturally saw each other regularly, and I talked with them. They were always together—mother and daughters. Whatever discord you might infer from the diary was swept away now by existential need. They were always together. It is certain that they gave each other a great deal of support. All the things that a teenager might think of her mother were no longer of any significance.

What I mean is that there are people who talk about the war, whose bike was requisitioned, how terrible that was, and then they stop. For them, that was the very worst that happened. If you say, "Yes, but there are people who went into hiding, and, much worse, there were also people in the camps."

"Oh yes, that was too bad, but I had to give up my bike."

I think it was that way with Anne. When she was in hiding, which was a very unhealthy situation, her mother was some-one against whom she rebelled. But in the camp, all of that

129

actually completely fell away. By giving each other mutual support, they were able to keep each other alive—although no one can fight typhus.

There were other groups in our vicinity. In fact, there were very few people on their own. I remember that there were two women in Libau who were alone and they formed a group. Because you see, a camp puts demands on you that are unthinkable in normal life. All of us in our group met that test—gloriously. That creates a bond that you can't compare even to that of sisters and mothers; it goes beyond that. That is the positive thing about such an experience.

Within that group of eight, there were subgroups. Anita and I were the two youngest; we were clearly the children. Nettie and Lydia were the two oldest. For us they functioned as camp mothers and we were their daughters. Lenie was especially close to Annie, and Rosy was mostly with Rootje. Stealing from one another was completely unthinkable; on the contrary, if one of us got an extra piece of bread, it would be divided into eighths. Everyone got a bit, however absurd that may sound. And although no one benefited from that physically, it was a psychological boost.

Another example: Anita didn't have shoes anymore, and toward the end, I had a friend—well yes, a friend, a poor thing. He was a French slave-laborer in the factory who sometimes slipped me something, which was promptly divided into eighths, and I asked him for a pair of shoes for Anita, which he got for me. I set them under Anita's bed—they were a pair of men's shoes. She saw them suddenly, as a kind of miracle from heaven. She put them on. It's funny, but she only learned a short time ago that I had put them there.

I was fortunate enough to have a warm dress. Once, after a turn at the showers following a selection, we all had to throw our clothes in a heap and they were arbitrarily thrown back. Rosy saw my dress lying there and she ran to get it. She got a lash with a whip for doing that, but she had the dress, and she gave it to me.

Not long ago, someone told me that I had once given her a piece of bread, a portion of bread, and they still talk about it. I don't remember. To give someone a slice of bread doesn't seem something special, But then it was a something very grand.

———

My memory of the liberation outshines everything. We didn't have any more work in the factory where we previously had made tire chains because there were no more deliveries of material to make them. So we were recruited, with our exhausted bodies, to construct an airfield, with shovels, huge shovels, and we also had to endure a lot of physical abuse. During the final weeks of the war, in the first days of May, in continuous rainfall, we had to construct that airfield, but a rumor spread like wildfire that Holland had been liberated. And it was true, but we didn't know that.

At one point, because everything was completely soaked, we were sent to the barracks. A couple of Dutch boys from the factory, Frans and Bert, walked by in the sandy street that went along the camp and to the melody of "Piet Hein" (a heroic Dutch folk song) They sang: "We are freed, the liberation is at hand, and tomorrow, we'll be free."

We ran outside to hear what they were saying because, of course, they weren't allowed to come into or near the camp, but that's how they let us know. And we repeatedly called out, "They are singing; they are singing that the war is over."

The day passed. Finally, the weather was beautiful the morning of the eighth of May, and we had roll call. It was rather strange. The one who took the roll, the *Lagerälteste* (senior camp guard), stood with her back to us, and the one who announced the number of *Häftlinge* (prisoners) stood there grinning. There was a great commotion in the guardhouse that was the entrance to the camp. We stood at roll call for a very short time. Then we were allowed to return to the barracks, and at a certain point, we saw them leave. Very soon thereafter the

131

slave-laborers—the Dutchmen and two Frenchmen—entered the camp. We were free! We could go in and out! The impossible had happened: The war was over and we were free! I felt myself growing; in one way or another, I got taller. I stood up straight, I think, and I lifted my head up high, and I stretched.

I have always considered that to be the most beautiful day of my life: To stretch and feel your body and, with your face turned to the sun, to have it penetrate that it was all over, that you had made it. All of that was simply impossible to comprehend, that intense feeling of happiness sweeping over you because you had survived and they were gone. You couldn't think of anything beyond that. And do you know what we did? Those sloping piles of sand next to the barracks, which we had always had to be so precise about, piling them up neatly and smoothing them with our hands—we jumped into them.

And from that moment on, everyone said, "Bloeme always said, 'on the first day of May . . .'" I had, after all, dreamed that in November.

A feeling of guilt—survival guilt—I don't have that at all. It is impossible to feel that you are guilty because you were able to escape the fate of almost everyone else. I don't feel any guilt for it. I consider it all as dumb luck, as an inexplicable outcome.

I am happy that I didn't share that fate. That gave me the opportunity to bring a new generation into being. If there is any sense in my coming back, then it is that Hans and I have been able to raise a relatively large family, and that our children have also had children. In that way, we have contributed and have given shape to the continued existence of the Jewish people.

Despite everything, there was room in the camp for some humor. That was because we were optimists, and I am sure of that. Above all, I want to bring to promote and encourage the best in all people. Somehow, I have never lost my naive trust in people. Actually, I think that's strange, but that's how it is.

Some anti-Semites, the moderate ones, say, "Well, I don't like Jews, because a Jew once cheated me." Those are stereotypes. In the first place, I don't believe it, and secondly, I am not convinced of their good intentions.

When I'm ready for a fight I say, "Christians killed my whole family, murdered all of my people, and not just now, but throughout the centuries, but I don't hate Christians."

I also have a pessimistic side, when I see that people are full of aggression and that it hasn't diminished over the centuries. Archaeological excavations testify that people were murdered in the past. In the Bible, one of the first acts of the new human race was the murder of a human being. The development of technology makes it possible to destroy an increasing number of people at one time. Thus, at the micro level, I am an optimist, and on the macro level, I am a pessimist.

LENIE DE JONG-VAN NAARDEN

Lenie de Jong–van Naarden.

M y first meetings with Lenie de Jong were always in the company of Bloeme Evers. Their survival together was the basis of a very close friendship.

Comradeship means a great deal to Lenie. She and Bloeme Evers-Emden, Anita Mayer-Roos and some other women formed a group and helped one another to survive the concentration camps.

Lenie's husband was in Auschwitz with Otto Frank. After liberation by the Russians, they returned to Holland but only after a long and arduous journey, via Odessa to France by ship, and then to Belgium.

Lenie is a sensitive woman, warm and engaging, and I was conscious of the emotions that our conversations released. She wanted to tell her story. And she did, speaking very carefully, weighing each word. Lenie told of her experiences in a way that deeply affected me.

To this day, Lenie does not understand why she survived. As she says, "It was the end of everything. Really the end of everything. That we came through it is a miracle. Very religious people understand it better than I do. I have never understood it."

Lenie de Jong—van Naarden

We were married in August 1942, in the middle of the war. It actually wasn't our intention to get married then, because my parents-in-law, who lived in Antwerp, had fled to the south of France. We no longer had contact with them and we would have liked so much to have had them with us there. But the laws were getting stricter all the time, so we said, "We're getting married."

By that time, we couldn't go to the town hall; so our marriage took place in the building that housed the Jewish congregation on the Plantage Parklaan. That day, we couldn't take the streetcar because at that very time, there were raids. We had to walk. The official from the registry who conducted our marriage ceremony gave a wonderful speech. He gave us courage. He probably realized that we would need it.

In the beginning of 1943, we had to go into hiding. Until the end of 1943, we were hiding in the Hague with a nephew of my husband. Then the entire situation was given away, and we just got on the train to Amsterdam and went to a very good friend of ours who had always said: "If something goes wrong, come here. But you can't stay; you can be here for only a while."

We did indeed stay there several months, waiting for an address in Friesland. Finally, that came through, and our friend took us to Friesland, near Joure, I believe. We arrived there on the stroke of eight, just as everyone had to be indoors. It was agreed that we would be picked up. And in fact a car arrived with a German license plate and dimmed headlights. We thought, Oh God, what now? It stopped. My husband gave the password, and the three of us got in. Two young men from Friesland sitting in the front seat immediately gave us American cigarettes. They really didn't want to have our friend join us, but we were able to explain the situation and so he was brought to another farm, from which he left very early the next morning to return to Amsterdam.

We drove farther in the car. Somewhere in the middle of the open country, the young men said to us, "Get out now; walk over to that tree, behind it there's someone who will take you with him." And that's how it went. We came to a farm, a sort of in-between address where a farmer and his very pregnant wife were waiting for us with a huge table already set. They said, "Take whatever you like—coffee, tea, and so forth." It was all on the table. We stayed there for one night. A few weeks later, we heard that the Nazis had shot the farmer.

The next morning, we were picked up in the same car, and taken to the Marine Police, in Delfstrahuizen, a place I had never heard of. We stayed there a couple of days.

In March or April, we went to our permanent address, in the vicinity of Oosterzee, to stay with a working-class family in a very tiny house. They were young people, our age, with two little girls. The house was very primitive, there was no water or electricity, and my husband had to pulverize carbide for a lantern which provided light. Water had to be rationed by the mouthful for meals; it was fetched from a farmer in the neighborhood. Water for washing came from the ditch. But none of that mattered. Those people were terrific and we got along with them very well.

Friends who were in the resistance movement came to visit us there, and they said, "You have to have a cellar to hide in." It was, after all, a little house that stood in a meadow. You could easily see through it from the front to the back. We constructed the underground shelter: a hole in the ground that was a sort of cellar, beautifully camouflaged.

In the beginning of August 1944, I was awakened by people walking around the house. I knew immediately that something was wrong. Right away, my husband and I leaped out of bed and dashed into the shelter with our protector. They went inside and we heard them walking above our heads. After some effort, they found us and broke through the floor above us. We came out in our night clothes and stood there facing Dutch SS men who said, "Quick, get dressed and come with us." And they told our *onderduikbaas* (the man whose house we had been hiding in), "You're going, too."

We got dressed and were allowed to take only a few things with us. We left immediately and went to Lemmer by bicycle, in the night. They had made the wife of our *onderduikbaas* stand outside in her nightgown and, with a revolver pointed at her breast, had threatened to kill her if she didn't tell where we were. But she hadn't said anything. When I had a minute to talk with her, she said, "I would never have betrayed you; I would have let them shoot me."

In Lemmer we were taken to the German police at the police station where they interrogated us. They registered us and afterward we went to Heerenveen with the bus and from there to the prison in Leeuwarden.

We were registered again there. We had to hand over our possessions—watches and wedding rings. My husband and our *onderduikbaas* were locked up in the section for men.

I landed in the women's section in a cell with an old woman, who subsequently went with me on the same transport. We didn't stay there long—a couple of days and nights.

Of the attendants in the prison, one was very friendly while the other was less so. Still, they did what they could to make life a bit bearable. The night before the transport, one of the women guards said, "Madam, I am putting you in a cell with Mrs. _____." (I don't want to give the name.) That woman had connections in the Leeuwarden court of justice. She was arrested because she had had a professor from Holland (the province of Holland) in her house. The guard let me spend that last night in the cell with her so that we could exchange some information. This woman, an extraordinary woman, said, "I was arrested because Professor so and so was in my house, but I will be set free; they are working on it. But you, unfortunately, are going on the transport." She was a good Christian, and she gave me a great deal of courage. Before I left, the guard gave me a large bowl of water so I could wash myself. I had very few clothes. The next morning, the guard gave me a loaf of bread to eat on the way, for which I was grateful. She said, "Here, maybe you'll need this."

The next morning, we were assembled downstairs. I saw my husband again there. Our *onderduikbaas* stayed behind in Leeuwarden in the cell. The Dutch SS men were there again, downstairs, and they put handcuffs on us. My husband and I were handcuffed, as were an old woman and an old man and Professor Freida, as well as a lot of other people. Early that morning, we walked through Leeuwarden, handcuffed—as if we were the worst criminals—accompanied by Dutch SS men. That's how we went to the train. There was practically no one on the street, it was outrageous that this should be possible, that there was no one to extend a hand to that group of Jewish people, young and old, and that we were left like that to our fate.

We were put in a section reserved for us on the train and taken under guard to Assen. We got out there, still handcuffed, and stood for a while a little apart from the train to wait for another train that was supposed to arrive, and when it came a lot of people of all ages got off.

The policeman who was awaiting us in Assen saw us hand-

141

cuffed and said to the SS man, "Take those handcuffs off." But the SS man replied, "No, no, those people are going to stay handcuffed." The policeman from Assen wasn't in uniform. A huge argument broke out between them. The Assen policeman said, "Come on, hand over the keys and unlock the cuffs on those people. We'll die of embarrassment going through the streets with these people this way." After considerable argument, the handcuffs were removed and we were brought, with a large group of people, to the prison in Assen.

What felt especially good was that they were waiting there for us with warm pea soup. I have never forgotten that. There were so many kinds of people in that time. The people in Assen did what they could. They didn't stuff us into cells, they let us sit together in one room, let us talk with each other, gave us pea soup, asked if we would perhaps like some more. They couldn't do anymore. At noon, we were already in large police vans which took us to Westerbork.

When we arrived there, we were registered for the umpteenth time, but since we were convicts, we ended up in the "S" barracks, the punishment barracks, where the men were separated from the women. The distance between the women's and the men's barracks was not great. During the day, I could see and meet with my husband.

The barracks were crammed full. We had to assure ourselves of a little place, a bed. In the meantime, I had made friends with a woman who was my age. We immediately became very close; it clicked between us, and we stayed together. And so we were together in an upper bunk. The barracks was very dirty, it was full of people, and it was infested with fleas. Whatever you had, you put on the bunk bed and you kept your clothes on so the fleas wouldn't bother you quite so much.

We were put to work on the batteries, in a workplace where we had to remove the brown coal from the batteries. We had already gotten a pair of overalls—dark blue with a red top— and wooden clogs. We had to turn in our own clothes at the entrance. Every day, we had to line up to go to the battery section. We were covered with brown dust which blew around and had to be collected in large cans. It was awful. We didn't have any soap. Someone from the *vrije* barracks (for those who weren't political prisoners), who had heard that my husband and I were in the "S" barracks, was able to slip a piece of soap to us. That was marvelous at that time. We were able to wash ourselves; there was plenty of water.

In addition to the work on the batteries, which kept a large group of people occupied, there were, of course, other work duties: work in the kitchen, cleaning the barracks, cleaning the streets, which were only dirt and sand but which had to be neatly swept, especially for official visits when everything had to look perfect. Everyone was given as much work as possible.

Official visits—that's when the bigwigs came, that is, the Germans and their Dutch side-kicks. At that time, they were Gemmeker and Van Dam, I think. They were the people who checked to see if the beds were made according to regulations and that sort of thing. When *Achtung* (attention) was called, you had to stand in a military position and they checked all over to see how things looked.

Those who were ill couldn't simply stay in their beds, they had to go to a hospital. But you were very careful not to stay in bed. As long as you could, you stayed on your feet.

In Westerbork, we quickly got to know a lot of people. After all, we were in the same boat, and there was a kind of feeling of togetherness. There were women with their husbands. Some of them had children with them. There were nephews, nieces, grandmothers, grandfathers; some of them had been picked up as entire families and all taken to Westerbork. It was a mass of people packed together, but we did get food regularly. The food was, of course, not very good, but it was there, and that was very important. Unfortunately, pregnant women or mothers with small children didn't get what they needed.

We knew, of course, that we would eventually go on the transport, but we didn't know where the transports went. We knew that Westerbork wasn't the final destination; but we had

143

no idea of what it would be like farther along. If we had been able to stay in Westerbork until the end of the war, it would have been a blessing, even with that crowded mass of people and under those conditions.

Naturally, we had heard the name Auschwitz, but it didn't mean anything. We didn't take it lightly, but what it meant exactly, and where it was, that we didn't know. Somewhere in Poland, nothing more. In fact little notes had came back in the cattle cars, a few words written about their arrival, but word of that came from so many different sources, almost anything could have been added to it. So we just waited it out. We were, in a way, resigned to what they wanted to do with us. Who knew what was in store for us all.

In Westerbork, I met the Frank family for the first time. My husband had quickly made contact with Otto Frank and got along with him very well. They had profound conversations and we had a very good relationship with Mrs. Frank, whom I always addressed as Mrs. Frank. I never called her by her first name; she was really a very special woman. I had less difficulty saying "Otto." She worried a lot about her children. She was always busy with those girls. It is an especially close relationship—a mother with children.

Soon thereafter we went on the transport. Naturally, I spoke with the girls. Anne, especially, was a nice child. Your heart broke since they were so young and there was nothing you could do to keep them out of it. Those children expected so much from life. We did too, of course, but we were years older. I was twenty-seven or twenty-eight. My husband was thirty-one. But that was what was so tragic about everything. You couldn't do anything—absolutely nothing. We had to let happen what would happen.

It was probably for the best when parents were with their children, because I met mothers after the war who had lost their children, and I have often thought: Mother, why didn't you go into the gas chamber too; it would have been better. After the war, their lives were unbearable. I still know those

Judentransport aus den Niederlanden — Lager Westerbork

3.September

am Häeftlinge 194 .

301.	Angers	Isidor	30.4. 93	Kaufmann
302.	Angers	Leonard	13.6. 2o	Landarbeiter
303.	Franco	Manfred	1.5. o5	Verleger
304.	Frank	Arthur	22.8. 81	Kaufmann
305.	Frank	Isaac	29.11.87	Installateur
306.	Frank	Margot	16.2. 26	ohne
307.	Frank	Otto	12.5. 89	Kaufmann
308.	Frank-Hollaender	Edith	16.1. oo	ohne
309.	Frank	Anneliese	12.6. 29	ohne
310.	v.Franck	Sara	27.4. o2	Typistin
311.	Franken	Abraham	16.5. 96	Landarbeiter
312.	Franken-Weyand	Johanna	24.12.96	Landbauer
313.	Franken	Hermann	12.5. 34	ohne
314.	Franken	Louis	1o.8. 17	Gaertner
315.	Franken	Rosalina	29.3. 27	Landbau
316.	Frankfort	Alex	14.11.19	Dr.i.d.Oekonomie
317.	Frankfort-Elzas	Regina	11.12.19	Apoth.-Ass.
318.	Frankfoort	Elias	22.1o.98	Schneider
319.	Frankfort	Max	2o.8. 21	Schneider
320.	Frankfort-Weijl	Betty	25.3. 24	Naeherin
321.	Frankfort-Werkendam	Rozette	24.6. 98	Schriftstellerin
322.	Frijda	Herman	22.6. 87	Hochschullehrer
323.	Frenk	Henriette	26.4. 21	Typistin
324.	Frenk	Rosa	1o.3. 24	Haushalthilfe

With frightening precision, the Nazis kept a list of the names of the 1,019 people, among them the Frank family, who constituted the last transport to leave Westerbork on September 3, 1944, for the German extermination camps.

Otto Frank's office at 263 Prinsengracht,
where the Frank family went into hiding in
the Annex in the beginning of July 1942.
*   On August 4, 1944, following betrayal,*
German police, accompanied by Dutch
assistants, arrived in trucks at the door.

Since 1957, the Annex has been open to the
public as a museum. Thousands of visitors
from all over the world visit the Anne Frank
House.

De Groene Amsterdammer

Led by Karl Silberbauer of the SD, the car with the onderduikers *(those who had been in hiding) drove directly from the Prinsengracht to the headquarters of the SD in Amsterdam. Two school buildings had been requisitioned as the headquarters of the SD.*

The day after their arrest, the Frank family was transferred to the Huis van Bewaring, a prison on the Weteringschans. (Photograph taken in 1987.)

On August 8, 1944, the transport, including the Frank family, left Central Station in Amsterdam for Westerbork.

From the beginning of the arrest of Jews in the summer of 1942, the Westerbork camp in Drente was used as a transit camp: a part of the deportation machinery used to send Jews to different Nazi concentration camps.

The camp was guarded by Dutch civilian and military police. Between the summer of 1942 and the spring of 1944, 85 transports left Westerbork for the extermination camps, 19 for Sobibor and 66 for Auschwitz.

When the Frank family arrived on August 8, 1944, approximately 100,000 Jews had already been sent to the "East."

After a month in Westerbork, the transport with the Frank family left for Auschwitz-Birkenau on September 3, 1944.

Auschwitz-Birkenau in 1987.

After an exhausting trip of several days, the train—the last transport to leave Westerbork—arrived in Auschwitz on the night of September 5–6, 1944.

Directly after arrival at Auschwitz-Birkenau, the men and women were separated, and a selection took place on the platform.

Five hundred forty-nine of the people on the last transport, including all the children under the age of fifteen, were killed in the gas chambers of Auschwitz-Birkenau on the same day they arrived, September 6, 1944. Anne escaped this fate since, at fifteen, she looked somewhat older.

Roll call in the women's camp in Auschwitz-Birkenau.

By the time the last transport from Westerbork arrived, about two million Jews had been gassed. At that time, there were 39,000 women in the camp. Edith Frank and her daughters, Margot and Anne, landed in Frauenblock *(women's barracks) 29.*

At the end of October 1944, the Russians were 60 miles from Auschwitz. From that moment, a large number of transports left the women's camp of Auschwitz-Birkenau to go to other concentration camps. Some of the women went to the work camp, Libau. Here they were put to work in factories for the German war machine. Edith Frank stayed behind in Auschwitz. Anne and Margot were transported on October 28 to Bergen-Belsen, arriving approximately two days later.

Bergen-Belsen in 1987.

Bergen-Belsen was originally set up as a transition camp for Jews who were intended to be traded for Germans who were in areas outside Nazi jurisdiction.

There were no gas chambers in Bergen-Belsen, which was situated on a barren part of the Lüneburger Heide in northern Germany, but the living standards in Bergen-Belsen were so terrible, particularly in the last months of the war, that 10,000 people died there.

Bergen-Belsen was not prepared for the large transports that came from Auschwitz-Birkenau, as well as other concentration camps, at the end of the war.

For the television documentary, Hannah Pick-Goslar returned to Bergen-Belsen, where she had spoken to Anne several times in the beginning of 1945, shortly before Anne's death.

The women were first put into tents, and then, after heavy storms in the fall of 1944, transferred to small barracks.

These photos were taken by the British army, right after the liberation of Bergen-Belsen on April 15, 1945, several weeks after the deaths of Margot and Anne Frank.

Of the tens of thousands of inmates who died at Bergen-Belsen, most perished in the months immediately before liberation and the weeks that followed.

The statement given by Janny Brandes-Brilleslijper to Otto Frank in 1946, attesting to the deaths of Anne and Margot Frank.

women, with all of their sorrow. Women who lost a couple of children and their husbands as well, who have never recovered. In that regard, to go together as as a family was for the best.

In Westerbork, I met women who, just like me, were married, without children. Some of them were with relatives, parents and brothers and cousins. I continued to keep up with these women in Auschwitz. The whole group was simply drawn together intuitively, and it has stayed that way up to the present. These women—they all came back alone. They were widows after the war. Some of them had children who had gone into hiding in the Netherlands and that came out all right. There were two women among us who had been picked up with their whole families. But only the women returned— none of their families came back. Women seem to have greater endurance, to take the orders less to heart, and perhaps they are a bit more independent.

I also got to know Bloeme, actually a very special girl. She was alone and joined us eagerly. She was an affectionate young girl. You told each other a little about your life, and then it simply clicked. It was the same way with Anita. Anita was with her father, mother, grandmother, brother, and nephew. They were all in that cattle car together with us. Anita was certain that of those young men somebody would return. But Anita is the only one who came back. That is the saddest thing about the whole situation.

———

The transports always left on Tuesdays. It's possible that this last transport left on a Sunday, but I don't know that exactly anymore. Usually, the transports always left on Tuesdays. But now they were in a hurry, an enormous hurry. The evening before, the names of those who had been selected for the transport were called out. There was nothing that could be done about it. When I heard my name and my husband's name called, I cried. It was the only time. I never cried after that!

Early in the morning, we were taken to a very long train with many cars. Next to it were SS men with dogs as well as the commandant, who didn't move a muscle. Whatever happened they allowed to happen. We were pushed into the cars. Those who were sick were shoved inside on stretchers. There were old people who had trouble climbing up into those cars. It was a dreadful sight.

We ended up in the same car as the Frank family, perhaps because of the relationship that my husband had with Otto.

There was a little bit of straw on the floor of the car. You could stand or sit, if there was room. When it was filled with about seventy people, the doors were bolted on the outside. Near the top there was a little window with bars. A young man stood there and told us which direction we were going. There was a small candle in a can which hung from the ceiling and provided a bit of light. We had to do our business in a pail which was filled in the first hour and then spilled over. With seventy people it was a terrible mess, with everything soaking wet. During the trip, a couple of young men saw an opportunity to empty the pail through the crack between the doors. You can imagine how much it stank.

The train rumbled along at a terrible speed. Sometimes it stopped for several hours, and once in a while the doors would be opened. Most of the time, however, they stayed shut. The young man at the little window kept on saying, "Now we are at so and so," and he would name one place or another. "Everything's been shot to pieces, I can tell you; there's been some bombardment here." That gave us a great deal of satisfaction.

Afterward, we heard that the train had stopped because people in another car had sawed a hole through the floor of the car. While they were still in the Netherlands, they had dropped through that hole and let the train ride over them. A few people were successful. One woman lost her hands and one man lost an arm. In one way or another, they were given help in the neighborhood which they had crawled to. They got out of it alive.

146

But no one else escaped—it was impossible. I know that people jumped out of the transports, but they must have been on some kind of regular train. It wasn't possible to escape from a cattle car since it was bolted from the outside.

Mrs. Frank had smuggled out a pair of overalls, and she sat by the light of the candle, ripping off the red patch. She must have thought that without that red patch, they wouldn't be able to see that we were convict prisoners. Well what she did made no sense, because when we arrived in Auschwitz, we had to leave everything behind in the cattle cars. Even so, for her it was important and she got some satisfaction from doing it.

Many people, among them the Frank girls, slept leaning against their mother or father; everyone was dead tired. And then, the tension: what would happen next, perhaps the train would crash. There might be a bombardment; we were hoping for that. Nothing, nothing happened. Even though there was so much bombardment, and all those trains that people knew were running. Nothing happened to them. A lot of people slept. It was simply a death train. People died [while] under-way, and there were many who were dead when we arrived.

I believe that we were in those cattle cars for two days and nights. After the war, someone asked me, "Didn't you get anything to eat?" No, we didn't get anything, absolutely nothing. If we ourselves had had something with us, okay, but I don't believe we did. We had nothing.

The young man who stood by the window and who regularly kept us informed apparently knew the map of Europe very well. He said, "We are going eastward, we're going in the direction of Poland; therefore, we're probably going to Auschwitz." Perhaps it was a sort of protection, to keep all of the things that you were thinking to yourself, in order not to make someone else afraid, to keep your own feelings to yourself, and not to let yourself go. Whatever Auschwitz was, we still had to discover.

For example, there were some people in those cattle cars who had washed their sheets in Westerbork, hoping that these sopping wet sheets would be dry when we got to Auschwitz. You would see that without understanding it. All of us were convinced that the situation was hopeless. But nevertheless, I don't remember anyone who kept on crying or who went to pieces. The people were calm.

That was because we were Dutch and had never been confronted with all this. We discovered that later, with the Poles and the Hungarians. They were savvy women, who knew just how to duck work. They knew the methods of the anti-Semites and they were much better prepared than we were. We hadn't been hardened. In general, Dutch people melted like snow in the sun. The young and the old didn't have any chance at all.

A cattle car like that, with seventy people, didn't have enough room for everybody to sit or to lie down. But there was, nonetheless, a sort of respect for each other. There were young men who gave up their places to old people or to women so that they could stretch out their legs a little, or even sleep. I still think of that train trip often. Especially during the night, I often can't sleep because in my mind's eye I see those trains still racing through the night.

At a certain moment, the train slowed down and stopped. I don't remember if it was morning or evening when we arrived. The doors were thrown open. There was immediately a terrible shouting over the loudspeakers. Uniformed policemen and soldiers were all standing there. Everyone piled out of the cattle cars on top of each other: the dead, the sick, the children.

The screaming over the loudspeakers told us that we had to leave our baggage behind and that we had to line up with our hand luggage, women on one side, men on the other side, and get going. It was inhumane, degrading, how they guarded us, with whips, with dogs. It would have been better to have fallen down dead. But so long as you didn't do that, you had to move.

My husband and I said our farewells then, very quickly— they left us no time for anything. I went to stand with the women. The men stood on the other side. We walked toward Mengele with his lackeys. (We only later heard that it was

148

Mengele.) He said, "This side" or "that side." So, we went this way; a lot of people went to the other side, among them people I knew. We waved to each other and said, "So long," as if we would meet again. But we never again saw the people who were sent to the left side. Afterward, we understood that that had been a selection.

I had my period—that is often a matter of nervousness. I had had the chance to get a sanitary napkin from the car because I needed it. We came out of the selection as a thinned-out group and we stood around somewhere for hours. We saw fumes and smoke, but no one asked, "What could that be?" Men in striped suits came up to us, among them Dutchmen, and I remember that I asked one of them, "What is that, there in the distance?" And he said, "Oh, that has nothing to do with you. You are going to be quarantined. That's not for you; you'll get through."

We were dying of thirst and we were famished. We were taken to some large hall near a barracks when I heard Dutch being spoken. That was Annetje, who worked in the kitchen. She asked, "Are there any Dutch women here?"

"Yes," we said. She was a very nice girl.

She said, "Wait," and then she brought a container of red stuff—beet water, or something like that—and she gave it to us. We all took a drink.

Afterward, we had to line up in alphabetical order, and then we landed in front of a woman, an anti-Semitic Pole. She grabbed my left arm in a hard grip, twisted it around, and started stabbing it with a needle. That stabbing was painful. We still had our clothes on then.

Once the number had been tattooed, we were pushed along, to the outside. My watch and my wedding ring had been returned in the prison. I took the watch apart and stomped it into the ground (along with my wedding ring) because I had found out in the meantime that it would all end up with the Nazis. Maybe they did, but in any case the watch was broken.

When we were all standing together again with tattooed

149

numbers, we were directed to a large hall. "Take everything off." And all our clothes were thrown together in a pile. The women who had their periods kept something on, and when we were grouped together again, but naked now, they removed the hair from our heads with a pair of clippers. I had very long, pinned-up hair. All of the hairpins had to come out. I had them in my hand; the hair was on the floor. A bit farther on, stood other women and they had their body hair shaved off. They saw that I was still wearing something; they took that off and I had to figure out how to manage.

Afterward, we went to a large room. They announced that the only thing that we could keep was our shoes. We had to put them into a disinfectant at the entrance and leave them there. Then we had to go to the middle of the room.

Now I had very good shoes, sports shoes, and I was actually very concerned that nothing should happen to them, so I watched them very carefully. They were taken and a pair of pumps was put in their place. Because it was a life-and-death struggle, and since I thought that I wouldn't stand a chance of survival without my shoes, I went to an SS man, period and all, completely naked. They were walking around with whips and whenever one of those naked women—who were help-less—didn't please them, she got whipped. I said to that SS man, "*Befehl ist Befehl* (An order is an order)." You said that we could keep our shoes. My shoes were stolen." And he pushed me backward with his whip and looked me over from top to bottom.

He said, "Who did that?"

"That woman there," I said.

She was wearing my shoes. It was someone who wasn't in our group. She had some kind of function—I don't know what. He had her come up to him. She had to take those shoes off and set them down. The SS man struck her so severely with the whip that I don't think she survived. Look, there were so many things that you saw happen; one incident didn't stand out. They were busy with our extermination. She, too, was a

150

Jewish woman, who was, it seems, allowed to sweep the floor.

Afterward, we went under the showers, where, of all things, there was still a little water. Still wet, we were sent outdoors. We didn't have a towel or anything. There, they threw us a bundle of clothes. I had a torn pajama top, some kind of skirt, and nothing underneath, absolutely nothing.

But, you won't believe it: Again we stood for roll call. We were a sight to see with those bald heads. My period was very heavy, and an *Aufseherin* (guard) who supervised us slipped a sanitary napkin into my hand. She didn't look this way or that; she saw how it was with me. There were other women who were having their periods. Maybe they got something as well. I don't know. But I was so thankful to her.

We stood in rows at roll call. The rows had to be lined up precisely. You had to stretch out your arm, to measure whether the distance between everyone was equal, because when the SS came, they had to be able to walk in between the rows easily.

Only after we were standing there neatly did we get something to drink. Each row got a can filled with so-called coffee, some kind of brown liquid. And if I tell you now that there were women with high fever, their mouths completely dried you will understand that one took only one or one-and-a-half sips, because solidarity is very important under those circumstances. You didn't take more because then the woman behind you wouldn't have anything. We also got a piece of bread, a sort of sourdough bread, that was, at the same time, our breakfast. We had to make do with that until the following morning.

I am glad that my parents and the rest of my family went into the gas chambers immediately. That was for the best. They were spared a long martyrdom. They didn't know what was going to happen. Death came immediately and they were spared everything. But that struggle of the mothers with children, the children who were taken away from them, that was the worst, because those women still had to fit into a work routine, and that was more than horrible.

In one way or another, you discovered that people were

151

being gassed, that there were rooms into which people were driven and then the doors were closed. We thought very often, Now, it's our turn. Well it didn't happen, for whatever reason.

I can tell about one time. We were put into a large barracks with every possible nationality mixed together. One day, all of those barracks were emptied. You have to imagine that there were at least fifteen hundred women in such a barracks, with very long corridors, with three stacks of beds one above the other, with twelve women next to each other in each of them. Beds—well now, that is too elegant a word, they were planks—with horse blankets, which you could lie under or on top of. We were always lying next to each other in groups of ten or twelve, like sardines in a can.

Such a barracks was enormously large. And completely filled with women with numbers on their arms. We were happy with those numbers because we thought that at least we had been registered. But that was completely wrong. New arrivals came in great numbers, so they could fill the gas chambers regularly.

But that night, we were lying on the beds and we heard automobiles driving back and forth. Women were being forced to get into the cars. The camp or *Lager* senior—as she was politely described—in our barracks was a Russian political prisoner, not a Jew. How did we know that? Everyone had one kind of "mark" or other, from which we could see whether she was a murderer or a political prisoner or simply a Jew. She opened the doors of the barracks, in the front and in back. It was pitch dark outside. All you could see was the barbed wire that was constantly electrified because all the lights there lit. We were dead still and then saw the Russian camp senior go from bed to bed and then quickly hide in the passageway again. Each time she said a few words to the women. When she came to us, she said the words, *"Seid bitte ruhig* (Please be quiet)," and then she went to the next bed. The trick worked! Because of that, they forgot to empty that entire barracks.

While the cars drove on toward the other barracks and we remained deadly still, I heard a large group of French girls outside, singing the "Marseillaise." That is how they went into the gas chamber.

I think that Russian herself was killed. She was an ordinary political prisoner. Oh, the hatred they had for the Russians was at least as great as that for us, if not greater. After all, they were at war with the Russians and those politically active women who had resisted—they didn't like them at all. That courageous woman saved our lives.

Older girls who could still be expected to be productive as workers, could stay with their mothers. That is why Margot and Anne Frank stayed with their mother. But most of the mothers had to surrender their daughters. They were always asking, "Do you know where my child is? Do you know?" And I always said, "No, I don't know, but we can't let it get to us; we have to try to get through it. Just hope for the best." I knew that mothers with children were the worst off. Women who were pregnant didn't have any chance at all. Many women threw themselves against the electrified wire fence.

As an individual, I think, one didn't have a glimmer of a chance. Maybe there are people who say now, "I am glad that I was alone; that is how I got through it." But for me, that didn't apply, and it didn't apply to our little club either.

In the period that we were in Auschwitz—about two months—Mrs. Frank tried very hard to keep her children alive, to keep them with her, to protect them. Naturally, we spoke to each other. But you could do absolutely nothing, only give advice like, "If they go to the latrine, go with them." Because even on the way from the barracks to the latrine, something could happen. You might walk in front of an SS man by accident, and your life would be over. They simply beat people to death. It didn't make any difference to them. A human being was nothing.

The work that we did consisted of dragging stones from one end of the camp to the other end. Why that was necessary, heaven knows. There was another group who brought the stones back. We had to work. But we didn't hurry. We did obediently bring the stones to the men who needed the stones, but we still always tried, even without words, to delay it a little. We said to each other, "Let him drop dead." And, "Don't go so fast." We kept up a very slow tempo. Later, too, when we worked in the factory in Libau, making tire chains, we always did something or other so that the machines would break down. Nothing was said; it happened spontaneously.

We were always together in Auschwitz. All in our little club did the same work, dragging stones. We were always more or less together. We didn't walk close together, of course, but we kept our eyes on each other, and when we could go back into the barracks, then we snuggled together again.

Fear, of course, also has a limit. There was only one thing that could happen to us and it was that we would have to go to the gas chamber, but we couldn't constantly think of that. When it got to that point, good, then there was no escape, then we probably wouldn't have panicked, then we would have given up the struggle. Gradually, we nevertheless reached the end of our rope. In Auschwitz, you abandoned all hope. You didn't have the illusion that you would ever get out. Only when we were finally on the transport again and could leave that place behind us did we get a little more hope.

You couldn't avoid anything—nothing. They thought for you. It was not expected that you would think of anything yourself, because if you did, then it couldn't be carried out; thus, if you had thoughts you shared them with your friends, but otherwise with no one. And no one ever asked, "What do you think of these circumstances?"

After two days in Auschwitz, all our feelings had already disappeared. We tried to keep that from happening through our conversations. We told about our lives and about our husbands and how everything had been. That's how we filled the time when we weren't sleeping.

The hygiene in Auschwitz was abominable. There was water, if you could get to it. In the mornings, the Nazis expected us to stand in neat rows of five, with our hair combed, washed and clean, but we didn't have anything. Water did come out of the faucets, but there were signs with skulls and crossbones everywhere. Maybe it was indeed poisoned, but I know for certain that I drank the water. We were dying of thirst. Each day our food was a piece of bread, sourdough bread; sometimes we got a small dab of butter as well, sometimes also a teaspoon of honey in your hand. Annie and I always shared our portions in the mornings and evenings. At most, it was a slice and a half of bread. It was very minimal, and later there was even less.

I remember that Anne Frank had a rash and ended up in the *Krätzeblock.* She had scabies. Margot voluntarily went to stay with her. Those two sisters stayed with each other, and the mother was in total despair. She didn't even eat the piece of bread that she got. Together with her I dug up a hole under the wooden wall of the barracks where the children were. The ground was rather soft and so you could dig a hole if you had strength, and I did. Mrs. Frank stood next to me and just asked, "Is it working?"

"Yes," I answered.

I dug close in under the wood, and through the hole we could speak with the girls. Margot took that piece of bread that I pushed through underneath, and they shared that.

Shortly thereafter, we went on the transport and they stayed behind. Later they were sent, sick, to Bergen-Belsen. At least, Anne was sick. We knew that already. Mrs. Frank didn't go with us on the transport, nor did she go with the children. She stayed behind in Auschwitz.

In the barracks where they were, women went crazy, completely crazy. There were people who threw themselves against the electric fence. Not that we endured it easily, but perhaps we could let off steam in one way or another by talking to each other. To work it out completely alone—that didn't work; even very strong women broke down.

Auschwitz was really the end of everything; the clay soil always with standing water; a huge quagmire without a sprig of green. No fly flew there. Not a bird, of course, nothing. There was nothing, nothing that looked alive, no flower, nothing, absolutely nothing. It was the end of everything, really the end. That we came out of it is a miracle. Very religious people understand it better than I do, because I never understood that a higher being—if one exists—could let all of this happen.

I myself have never believed in God. Maybe I had a direct approach. I am a sort of Tevje, who calls God to account at the moment that it suits me. I have indeed thought that. In fact I did that in Auschwitz. I called God to account. "God, are you allowing this to happen?" I never got an answer and nothing changed. Religion—you get that with your mother's milk, I've always said. In my surroundings, in our little club, there was just one woman who remained religious through thick and thin. She never omitted her morning and evening prayers. She stood facing the east and we shook our heads. "How can she do that?"

In September, after our arrival, was the period of the Jewish high holidays. With the Day of Atonement approaching, a group of Polish Jews came up with the idea of asking them to postpone the distribution of bread from one evening to the next evening. "Could we, perhaps, get the piece of bread that we get every evening together with the piece we get tomorrow?" The result was that we got nothing. And I would have gladly had that piece of bread.

We talked with each other about the atmosphere at home and what would be served on the table after the fasts. But it was also grim on the holidays. If they could torment us a bit more, they certainly didn't lose the opportunity. So we got nothing at the end of the Day of Atonement.

After the umpteenth selection, we knew that we were going on the transport again to Libau. We were shaved again and disinfected again. They pushed a cloth of stinking stuff under your arms and down below, to kill your lice. I got a light-blue silk dress and a coat, which didn't fit. Still, we got something for the cold! Because, they told us, we were going to a work camp.

We thus got through the selection again; again that same Mengele with his lackeys. Again we stood neatly lined up, but Nettie wasn't there. We were desperate because it was so life-threatening for us, but of course, primarily for her.

Where was Nettie? We stood there for a while. Then suddenly we saw Nettie, completely naked, carrying a little bundle, a finger at her lips. She had been stuffed into the cubicle where all the women went before they went into the gas chamber. When the door opened again to throw the next one in, she crept out under the arms of the SS man and took off. She had filched a bundle of clothes and a jacket. These were perhaps the happiest moments of my life because we couldn't live without each other. Without each other, we would have gone to pieces. Our mutual solidarity was so great. We didn't want anything to happen. We knew that Nettie had children. They were in Holland. Her husband didn't come back. We only heard that later, of course. But again and again our first thought was of the children who had to see their mother again.

Nettie was a very warm person. I was very sick in Auschwitz, with a high fever, and Nettie said to me, "Leen, the only thing I can give you is a little of my body warmth. Crawl right up next to me and tomorrow you'll be better."

I did get better. Later, we always said, "If you have the chills, then go outside and stand in the rain, completely naked, shave your head bald, and then you'll get better."

For our departure for Libau in Upper Silesia, we got bread and a winter coat. At the distribution there wasn't so much a feeling of celebration as there was one of growing reassurance. Something like, "Who knows, we may survive. . . ."

We went to Libau in the same cattle cars, but that feeling of growing reassurance stayed with us. During the trip which lasted for hours, we were accompanied by soldiers, SS men, I think, who were as friendly as could be. But we didn't want to take anything from them. In their baggage, they had sausages and cheese, and they offered them to us. We didn't take anything, although we naturally had a craving and were very, very hungry.

They opened the doors of the car a little. We were going through a beautiful area. In the meantime, it had become a snowy landscape—Silesia was a kind of Switzerland. I will never go there again, but it was a very lovely area.

When we finally arrived, German women were waiting for us near the train. They were really friendly, of a sort that we had never encountered. The barracks were in a kind of valley. We did see chimneys smoking, but we were reassured; these were stoves burning. The stoves were going when we were divided into barracks groups, but after that they were never lit again.

The hell of Auschwitz lay behind us, which isn't to say that we were completely safe. There was a young girl with us, the same age as Anita and Bloeme, who got sicker and sicker. She coughed and coughed, and the little food that we could get for her, she couldn't eat. We were so famished. She said, "You can eat it, or don't you dare? I have T.B."

We said, "Of course, we'd dare to eat it. Give it to us, and we'll eat it later." It was soup with a lot of water in it. She had eaten a spoonful of it, and we calmly ate the rest. Each of us had one spoonful of it.

Finally she was taken to the hospital, which was a bit better than the one in Auschwitz. It was a stone barracks, across from the camp where we were. You had to ask a soldier or an SS man for permission to visit your sick sister—we always called her our sister—and then you would get permission to cross the narrow path to visit briefly. By then we were already working in a factory, and we pulled a piece of cardboard off a box, we filched a pencil, and we all wrote something on the piece of cardboard. Whoever went to see her hid it under her clothes. All of that had to be done on the sly, but we did it. Oh, she was so sick. One of us read some of it to her and she laughed. Later, she died.

We had to bury her ourselves, which in itself indicates that matters there were a bit more humane. We got a hand cart and we got a casket from a casket factory which was nearby. We laid Tetta in that. We brought her through snow and ice to the cemetery, but she had to be buried outside. A hole had already been dug, in that very stony and frozen ground. They helped us lower the casket into the hole with a rope.

After the war, we placed a marker on her grave. We simply commissioned someone—then the roles were turned around, weren't they?—and said, "You have to make a sign with this name and the date of death on it." She was the daughter of a cantor from Leiden, and I wanted to have her body brought to the Netherlands after the war, but a religious woman in our group said, "That isn't done. What is in the ground, we leave there. Tetta was a religious girl and that isn't permitted." I went along with that.

In the meantime, many women had died. You didn't stay alive there either! Not only because of the severe climate, but also because the work was too hard. We were constructing a landing field on the other side of the mountains. Very early in the mornings we walked up the mountain, then down the mountain to a field where it was ice cold, and either snowing or raining. Many women fell and couldn't stand up again; they died.

There were five hundred women, all fit for work, who had been selected for that—not only Dutch women—but many who were not Dutch. In the beginning, we worked in a factory making tire chains for the SS cars. We had, of course, a lot of difficulty putting them together the right way. Each chain weighed I don't know how many kilos. Annie and I made the final check. Afterward, they had to be thrown in cardboard boxes, and we said, "Everything is in order, hup, put them in." The chains were put together from tiny pieces of chain, on an assembly line, and finally, in one way or another, they were made to fit around a car tire.

We also cleaned up—we swept the halls of the factory and scrubbed the toilets. That is to say, we scraped ice. We had to see to it that they were cleaned, with practically nothing to clean them with. Sometimes we threw sawdust on the floor, which we had to get at the casket factory. And with our bald heads, where just a little sparse hair grew, we looked terrible. There was also a Frenchman who worked in the factory and when we, by chance, went to the w.c.'s at the same time, he would open the door, saying "*Après vous, Madame* (After you, Madame)." We were so filthy that no one would touch us with a ten-foot pole, but that made us feel a bit like women again.

We knew that the war was coming to an end. Look, we had a *Lagerälteste*, a shrew, and one day she said to us, "You all have to work, but I will do everything I can to keep you here, because there are a great many women who are already walking through the snow from the East, because the Russians are advancing. But I will do everything to keep you here so that you don't have to go through the snow." That was clear. Just the same, she let us stand in the snow, which came up to your knees and higher. Thirty degrees below zero (centigrade) was quite normal. To protect myself against the cold, I had a warm silk dress and a coat, but no stockings.

We sensed that something was going to happen, but what? You were isolated, you didn't hear a radio, no one told you anything. But a certain mood prevailed. At the end, we didn't work anymore. We were kept indoors. Naturally we heard continuous bombardments, coming closer, but we didn't know how close they were, since the mountains threw the noise back at us.

One day, Annie and I were picked out. We had to go outside to saw wood with a large handsaw. It was very primitive, sawing through thick blocks of wood. Heaven only knows why.

I said to Annie, "Let's push that thing a little farther and

160

then we'll be a bit closer to the fence. Perhaps some French workers will come along there." And indeed, a couple of French men, whom we knew from the factory, passed by, and they said, *"La guerre est finie* (The war is over).*"*

"What did they say?" Annie asked me.

I said, "They say that the war is over. That can't be; we're still working."

That was, I think, the sixth of May. At the end of the lane, they turned around once more and repeated it *"La guerre est finie"*—saying it as they went by because they weren't allowed to stand still.

Later, we returned to the barracks and told the other women.

Well, the seventh of May was already a strange jumble. On the eighth of May, we saw that the Nazis had left. I remember that Nettie, who had been selected and couldn't work any more in Libau, stood at the little window of the barracks and said, "Guys, the war is over."

I was sitting close to the little window and answered, "You're out of your mind," and we didn't do anything.

But then some women came, who said, "Hey, the Nazis are gone. The war is really over."

We went outside, but not outside the barbed-wire fence— we were so used to being behind barbed wire. Then the first Russian came.

An officer, or officers, with sickle and hammer on their caps, entered the camp. They gathered all the women who were there around them. They spoke German. The Russian officers spoke German or English, the ordinary soldiers only Russian. The officer was a Jew. He stood up on a stool—I will never forget that—and fired his pistol in the air. He said, "As you stand there, I promise you, we will take revenge. Believe it. You have been liberated by us." And afterward, we sang the "International," in many different languages—French, German, Dutch.

At noon, we could leave the camp. On the highway, an entire Russian army unit moved past us. Inconceivable—so

161

many wounded and so many terrible things. The tanks opened up, because they had to stop every few moments. Women came out of the tanks, three or four women per tank. They were terrific, really good, comradely people whom we met there. The first thing they did was to offer us pieces of bacon which they had in the cabins. But we didn't eat it, we couldn't eat it. It was too fatty. We only licked it.

Dutch people are a little slow to take the initiative. We weren't so great at organizing. That same day the Polish and Hungarian women ran into a farmer who had cans of milk in his wagon. They kicked the farmer off his wagon and returned to the camp with the horses and the milk. That was the first milk we got. But they also turned up with chickens under their arms, which were slaughtered at once. In no time at all, they had broken into the kitchen and made a pot of soup with chicken and so on. They were much handier in those matters than we were.

We also went into houses. We tried to satisfy our appetites, but we always came back with the wrong things, with loaves of bread. I know that I had a pile of bread that almost reached the ceiling, and Annie said, "We'll start with the one at the bottom." All those round loaves, you know, that you piled on top of each other, and we said, "Yes, but what shall we do with the top one, because that is so nice and fresh."

Except for Anita, Nettie, and Lydia, who went a different way, we returned on foot to the Netherlands. We walked for weeks—it is inconceivable. We stayed overnight with farmers. There were a couple of Dutch men with us who had worked in the same factory, and a couple of French men who came with us. There were about ten or twelve of us and we were taken in everywhere. Annie was the smartest of us all. She had the Russians give her a paper with a red stamp, a sickle and hammer, and that did wonders. The Germans were so afraid of the Russians, so terribly afraid, and we profited tremendously from that. The Russians stole right and left. Whatever there was to collect, in the way of watches, cameras, or interesting

162

things, they took for themselves. We naturally thought that that was wonderful.

We were only interested in eating. And we ate things that we couldn't tolerate at all, and then we had to stay somewhere in order to recover.

We arrived in the Netherlands in the beginning of July. Without help from anyone—not even the Red Cross—and without transportation, we had walked through the ruins of what had once been Germany. We were kept in Bunzlau for three weeks by the Russians. That was a center for English and French prisoners of war, who, like us, wanted to get to the West. At the end of June, we were in Leipzig with the Americans, who took excellent care of us.

My husband and I had agreed that if we should survive, we would go to our friend's house. When I arrived, my husband was already there.

My husband and Otto Frank were freed at Auschwitz. That was in January 1945. My husband's hands and feet were frozen and he said, "I'll never walk anymore and if they want to shoot me, then they can just shoot me here." There was a large group, including Otto Frank, who also stayed behind.

The liberation came quite unexpectedly, so he told me. They first had roll call for everyone who had stayed behind. They were the really sick, with frozen limbs and so forth. Then machine guns were set up. At that moment, when the inmates thought they would all be gunned down, the Russians entered the camp with small horse-drawn wagons.

Pretty crazy. And as quickly as my husband could tell about it, they were freed and the Nazis were gone or taken prisoner. They broke into the storehouses to get food; they were brimful. There were shoes, blankets, and clothes in abundance.

Just as we had, they got food from the Russians, but they didn't have much—mainly toasted bread. And they immediately got medicines from the medical orderlies. There were doctors too. My husband had frozen fingers on both hands and the doctor said, "I'm going to remove two fingers from each

163

hand." My husband still had all his wits about him and he said, "No, that isn't going to happen; nothing is going to be removed." Later on he always had trouble with his hands, he has been under treatment, but fortunately, he has been able to deal with it very well.

When they had recovered a bit, a group, including my husband and Otto Frank, started out, and after considerable wandering, they landed in Odessa. In Odessa, a large transport ship was ready to take them to the West—first, to France since there were quite a few French prisoners among them. My husband always talks about the wonderful reception in France.

Then they went in the direction of Holland. They first landed in Belgium. There, the reception was already a bit less wonderful. Finally they arrived in Holland. They had a paltry reception there—a single policeman who said, "Now guys, we're going with a group to Teteringen. I am bringing you to a farmer's house. You'll stay there until there is a way to get you where you have to go, to Amsterdam or whatever." The group disintegrated and everyone went his own way.

We women stayed together until we got to Maastricht. Then a vegetable truck took us to Amsterdam, to the Berlagebrug. I went to the address where my husband and I had hoped to find each other. When I rang the bell and our friend opened the door, he was speechless. Without saying a word, he took me into the room and pointed to my husband. For the second time in all that time, I cried—but now from happiness and thankfulness.

Our little club of women has stayed close all these years, right up to today. Without each other, we wouldn't have made it.

RONNIE
GOLDSTEIN-VAN CLEEF

Ronnie Goldstein–van Cleef.

Ronnie is a remarkable and talented woman. Her nearly emotionless but moving narration made a deep impression on me. The German concentration camps have left their mark, just as with the other women.

Her creative spirit kept her going. Her poems and drawings about the suffering in the concentration camps are more than therapy—Ronnie is an artist.

From the beginning of the war, Ronnie was active in the resistance. She worked as a courier, traveling all over the Netherlands by train. She also looked for hiding places for people sought by the Nazis, and she provided false identification papers. Ronnie was arrested after being betrayed.

It was in the Westerbork detention camp that Ronnie got to know the Frank family. She was on the same, fateful, final transport that left for Auschwitz on September 3, 1944. In Auschwitz, Ronnie shared many experiences with Anne Frank. They often stood together at roll call and they were together in the Krätzeblock where Ronnie sang to Anne and other children.

Ronnie Goldstein–van Cleef

I come from a very liberal Jewish family in the Hague. Although my father frequently went to Germany on business, he brought us up to be very anti-German. He always warned us about what might be coming, and when the Germans invaded our country, he said, "Now, we're finished." And then he quickly added, "But they'll never catch us."

We ended up, quite naturally, in the resistance; certain circumstances and requests from friends forced you to act. Already early on, we kept a printing press for the resistance hidden under the floor of our house.

On the first day that we had to wear stars, the mother of a friend of ours was picked up on the street. She disappeared during her daily walk. Since we didn't know what the reason for that could be, we removed all the things from her house that we thought might look suspicious to the Germans. That's how you tumbled from one thing into another.

One day her son and a couple of friends organized their own squad. I joined them as a courier and I was especially active after my father was arrested. My father was afraid that something would happen to me; he would have preferred that I hadn't done what I did.

After the raids in Amsterdam, my father had all our cousins come to the Hague and the entire family, including all the cousins, moved into a pension on R. van Goenstraat in one of those large houses. We stayed there for about three months, until we thought that it was quiet again, after which everyone went back home. Only a few of them were saved; the rest were taken away. When they got a summons, they found it too dangerous to go into hiding.

Our resistance group gathered in a photo shop on the Fahrenheitstraat in the Hague, the KIFO, where a girlfriend of mine was the manager. Behind that shop we had our meeting place, where we did all kinds of things, such as falsifying identity cards. We also arranged our appointments and rendezvous there. We reported there regularly, so that we would know that nothing had happened to any of us. When someone didn't show up at a certain time, we would all disappear, because then something was wrong.

You would automatically look for hiding places for people and try to make connections with people who could supply ration cards or registration certificates. Later, I came in contact with a young civil servant at the residents' registration office. He provided me with identification papers from city hall and passport photos from the municipal archives. Thus we could falsify papers and we could obtain papers from the crisis control services. These papers had an official seal and we could use them to legitimize people in hiding.

I ended up in the Nieuwe Nieuwstraat in Amsterdam with Aunt Dora, who had a great number of *onderduikers* in her house; she had a wonderful hiding place, an apartment that had been condemned, in which there were fourteen *onderduikers.*

I met Ans van Dijk there, who almost blew the whole thing. I was to take a boy to Twente. Aunt Dora knew Ans van Dijk from the time she was little and considered her to be completely trustworthy. Ans van Dijk asked if I could take another girl along. She gave me a picture of the girl, and I obtained an identity card for her. Later she proposed, "If you are at Central Station at such and such a time with that boy I will be there with the girl, and you can take both of them." That's what we agreed to do. At Central Station, I gave the boy my purse to hold because I wanted to get tickets at the ticket office. I turned around, I saw that the boy was being arrested, and holding only my change in my hand, I ran out of the station as fast as I could, jumped onto the streetcar, and went back to Aunt Dora's, where I burst into tears. I was so terribly shocked. Then I said, "That Ans van Dijk is not good; she is no good." And later that turned out to be the case. After the war, she was condemned to death and executed by the Dutch government.

In the meantime my parents went to Almelo. My father had once met a nurse on the train, and when the conversation turned to going into hiding, she said, "I live in a castle and we have enough room. Come stay with us." And my parents did. I was also there for a while, although it didn't seem quite so reliable as we had thought. The occupant of the castle had leased it from a steward who worked in the resistance.

The tenant proved not at all trustworthy. There was a raid at the castle on March 3, 1943, while my mother was out on a visit somewhere. My father had asked me to bicycle with him to Tubbergen. I said, "No, I'm not leaving. Just go by yourself." That is the last that I saw of him. Several hours later he was arrested. The cause for the raid, and also the arrest of my father, appeared to be betrayal by the tenant of the castle.

My father wanted to go to Tubbergen, to the Dr. Schaepmanshuis'—also a small castle, now a cloister and home for the elderly—to ask if they could take any *onderduikers* there, because we understood that the people in our castle had to leave. During my stay at the castle in Almelmo, I got to know Willem Mondriaan, who was the leader of a resistance group. I traveled for him, bringing people from the Hague or Amsterdam to Zwolle or to Almelo, from where Uncle Willem took them farther. I always got through a check on the train very properly. I had good papers.

It all went well until the middle of 1944. Our work consisted mostly of taking *onderduikers* away, caring for them, seeing to it that they got their identity cards, that they got their ration cards and registration certificates—in short, all of the papers that they needed. When new registration cards or stamps were issued, then we provided them. We also brought them extra ration cards after a raid. We had an unbelievably large number of ration cards at that time, and we distributed them so that the *onderduikers* could get extra food to eat and would be well fed. Almost all the people that I took into hiding survived. It is still very gratifying to realize that.

There were dozens of them. I don't know the exact number, but there were so many. Sometimes I was really very busy, because I took *onderduikers*—boys who were supposed to go to Germany as workers and didn't want to go—from Almelo to the Hague or to Amsterdam, where they were given further assistance.

I could move around freely. People thought that I didn't look so Jewish. I had light blond hair and I got through everywhere. I was afraid, but I had the will and courage. I don't know exactly—I didn't think about it further. It had to be done and I did it, even when it was very precarious, as it was with an old woman who actually didn't understand the whole situation and simply went on talking. I brought her to my mother, who lived close to the station in the Hague. I didn't dare to go on the street with that woman during the day. She was pretty well known since she had a lot of businesses. One morning, very early, when it was still dark, I picked her up from my mother's and took her on the train to Wierden, near Almelo. Upon our arrival, Uncle Willem said, "God, God, I wouldn't have done that," because the old woman really looked very Jewish. She survived and lived for years after the war.

———

171

In June, 1944, I was betrayed.

I didn't know it then, but since May I was being shadowed by the SD. I had a room in the Hague, on the Acaciastraat, a side street of the Laan van Meerdervoort. One morning, I ran into a girl who had been in school with me. She didn't have a coat, she was shivering, and her teeth had been knocked out. She was in a pathetic state. She called my name. It was near the last stop of the No. 12 (the streetcar line). I hadn't seen her for all those years, and I was terribly startled.

She said, "Can you help me? There was a raid at our place and I was able to get away. I don't have any shelter, I have no papers, nothing."

I said, "Of course I'll help you. Let's meet tomorrow evening, when it's dark and then I'll bring you an identity card."

She no longer had a registration certificate. I then went to the KIFO, the photo shop in the Fahrenheitstraat, and my girlfriend, who was the manager there and who also did courier work for us, said, "I don't trust this business. I don't think it's on the up and up." But I replied, "I know this girl very well. I used to go to her house. We biked to school together because we lived near each other."

I didn't see any harm in it. Late in the evening, we brought her to the house of my girlfriend. I told her, "Tomorrow I can get a place for you in Twente." But she didn't want that because she didn't want to leave her fiance in the Hague in the lurch. She simply wanted to go on walking around there. She used to drink a cup of *ersatz* coffee at Lensvelt Nicolaas in the Laan van Meerdervoort. We met there once. There was a mirrored wall there, and she suddenly said, "Oh, here comes Kaptein." He was an SD officer, a notorious one. I knew him by name, but I had never seen him. It really was him, and on that occasion, she actually pointed me out to him, as it were. Kaptein shadowed me from that time on.

In June I went to Amsterdam, where I was to pick up blank identity cards. I felt at ease because at that moment, I didn't have anything incriminating in my pockets. The train was packed, and I stood on the platform between the cars with many other people. And when they said, "They're checking the passengers on the train," I even thought, I'm in good shape here. They came to the threshold of that platform. There were two of them and they looked around. One of them said, "Yes, look, there she is." I looked around to see if they meant someone behind me, and I was quite scared. And then I had to go with them to another compartment where it became evident that they knew all about me. Then I said, "I don't understand at all what you are talking about." But I was terribly frightened.

They took me to Amsterdam, to the Euterpestraat, and I was interrogated there. At some point, I had a lucid moment. "I don't understand what you all want; I am Jewish, and I am looking for a shelter, because I don't have a room or anything, and I'm looking for some place to stay." And then they asked about my parents and I said, they were taken away a long time ago, in the beginning. Which wasn't true. My father had already been arrested then, but my mother, fortunately, had not.

And then I understood that I had been betrayed by that girl who had gone to school with me. Later, I was in Westerbork and I met acquaintances from school there. We talked about it and as we compared the circumstances of our arrests, her name came up in everyone's account. After the war, Kaptein was arrested and testified that he had forced her to do it. He protected her, and she was freed after a few months in prison. I didn't think she deserved such leniency.

After the war, Kaptein was condemned to death and executed because he had a lot on his conscience. I didn't know at the time that he apparently also mistreated my father. The investigating officer asked him, "And there was also a Mr. van Cleef from the Hague?"

"Oh, I beat him up," Kaptein said then. He had a memory like a steel trap, that man.

And when they said, "Yes, he also had a daughter."

He replied, "Yes, she was also picked up."

173

Then the investigator called me up. Kaptein was startled when I said, "And you made a mistake." Well, then I was able to testify against him and the man who presented himself as the investigator, Van de Ouderaa, who had been responsible for breaking up our group in the Hague.

I was brought from the Euterpestraat to the Huis van Bewaring (House of Detention) on the Weteringschans, where I landed in a cell with other women. In the end, there were forty women there. Every day, a few more came. Friendships were made because you wanted to help each other.

People reacted in different ways when they arrived there— some were bewildered, others relieved. "Hey, I'm glad that it's over." To live in hiding was naturally an enormous strain and tension for people. I remember that I slept awfully heavily and deeply the first night because an enormous weight had been lifted from my shoulders. But then you were seized by thoughts of what would happen next. You tried to figure out ways to escape. But there weren't any.

There were men next to us in another cell. We asked the guards if we could mend the men's socks. We got permission and used their socks to pass along information. I had my birthday at the same time as someone else and little notes were sent to the men in the socks. The men wrote poems and I got a very thick cigarette rolled together from stubs. I was very happy with that because I smoked an awful lot at that time. And I got a thick piece of bread and butter for my birthday. Yes, crazy. Then you realized what a strange circumstance it really was. The feeling of: Now, this can't last long. Soon, I'll be out of here. But all of that was naturally totally unreal.

After about ten days, we all had to leave our cells. We were to be taken to Westerbork. In front of the entrance to the prison, there were a couple of streetcars. We had written letters to our families and friends to let them know that we had been picked up. We asked the conductor of the streetcar if he would mail those letters for us.

"Yes," he said, "All right. Just put them all up there in the baggage net and I'll take them out in a little while." The SS or SD boarded the streetcar while it was standing still, and the conductor gave them all the letters. It was a packet, a whole stack of letters.

I have never been so angry. I was really furious. I thought, What a dreadful, stinker. He simply turned our letters over to the Germans, with the addresses that we had put on them. We had trusted him, to get the letters out on the sly, and he didn't do that. But later I learned that, fortunately, nothing awful had happened. Apparently they just destroyed the letters.

And so we went on a train to Westerbork. And there you were, sitting there in a somewhat cheerful mood, because you didn't understand any of it. On the one hand, sad, of course, but on the other hand, you don't know what they could yet do to you. You actually don't know anything.

In an office in Westerbork, one by one, we had to tell where we came from, who we were, if we still had any money or jewelry, if we had been in hiding, and so forth. Whether your parents were still alive. My mother was still all right at that time, but I said, "No, my parents have been gone for a long time." All of that was taken down. And then you went somewhere where your clothes were taken away and you got overalls and a pair of wooden clogs. And I thought, I'll never be able to walk with them, but they weren't so bad.

Then to the punishment barracks. In the time that we were there, in the summer of 1944, Westerbork was—to exaggerate somewhat—a bit of a vacation colony. We were well off there, but earlier, with a transport arriving every week, when thousands of people were there, it must have been awful. But in all the time that we were there, no transports left. I went there in the beginning of July. In September, the last transport left.

And during all that time, the weather was beautiful and we worked. I worked on the batteries. We had good food, we could get packages. We had chicken and Ovaltine and oatmeal—all good things. And we got good toothbrushes. There was a little store in the *vrije* camp and once in a while they let us get something from there. We got camp money. Naturally, you couldn't have used it for anything on the outside, but we could use it to buy things there. And so we were able to feed ourselves well.

I found Roger Goldenberg and Frits Heilbron in the camp. They had been in our group in the Hague. They had been arrested in May, betrayed by Van der Ouderaa, as was our unforgettable Kurt Reimer, who was picked up on September 3, 1943. Van der Ouderaa, who worked for the SD, was really named G. L. After the war, he was sentenced to seventeen years in prison for betrayal and collaboration. I had known Roger and Frits for a long time, so we took good care of each other. There was an enormous comradery, and when someone got a package, we shared it within our group, so we didn't suffer from hunger.

In Westerbork, I became acquainted with the Frank family. I found it remarkable that the entire family had gone into hiding together in one place. We had always made an effort to take children to different places, and also to separate married couples. Sometimes a husband and wife would be reunited later, but never an entire family. The risk was too great. When one of them was betrayed, then the whole family would be at risk.

The Franks were pretty depressed. They had had the feeling that nothing could happen to them. They were very close to each other. They always walked together. I didn't have very much contact with them; we greeted each other.

Transports arrived on a regular basis from Amsterdam and then we would go to see who had arrived—whether there were acquaintances or relatives among them. Fortunately, that wasn't so in most cases. But if you saw acquaintances, you said sadly, "How awful to see you here."

As soon as there were rumors about transports, everyone naturally became terribly anxious. We had already heard, after all, that Paris had fallen, and from that we assumed, Now, nothing more can happen to us, because they couldn't take us

176

very far—a bit of a feeling of reassurance that we would indeed stay there. That was, of course, not at all the case.

One night, someone came to the barracks from the Jewish camp police, with a German or an SS man, to call out the names. We were really so terribly tense, with knots in our stomachs, listening to see who was included. If you were included, then you suddenly didn't know what you should do. You experienced terrible dislocation and everyone consoled you: "Now, it won't come to that." And then people would say, "Auschwitz, no, that is no longer possible. Maybe Bergen-Belsen." The latter was, after all, not so far away, we thought. Actually, we didn't have any notion of what could happen.

The Frank family went with us on the transport. You were in a car, pushed into a cattle car, and you tried, as much as possible, to keep the people who were around you close to you so that you could give each other support. That worked most of the time. There were also a lot of old and sick people, who were brought into the car on a cart with very large wheels. I really didn't understand what they were doing with those people; we were, after all, going somewhere to work. And then I thought, Those poor people, these old people, they can't do anything anymore. And then an entire group of young children without their parents—who had gone into hiding or who had been arrested—this group also went into the cars. I have always had a hard time with regard to the children. That was always what was most upsetting to me. On the Weteringschans as well, darling children, three or four years old, were often brought in. We gave them an enormous amount of care and attention, but they went with us to Westerbork, and in the end they went along to Auschwitz.

We had never thought that we would go there. We didn't understand what it would really be like, we didn't want to believe it. Once in a while, a postcard would come from Buchenwald or from Mauthausen, and then we would think, Yes, people have to work very hard, but still we did get a sign of life from them. But that didn't mean a thing—they were really extermination camps. And we didn't comprehend that at all. It would be severe we thought, and the work would be hard. Now for that we were all prepared. But beyond that, that people would be murdered—I didn't expect that. Later, I was looking right at it, and even then, I doubted that it was true. It was not believable. Also, out of self-protection, I put on blinders and shut myself off from everything. I didn't want to experience it. I did, in fact, have a strong will to live and I thought: I will survive. I said that then, which was naturally very arrogant, because you actually couldn't know.

We left on the last transport from Westerbork. We were well aware that it would be the last one. We thought, after all, that the war would soon be over since the Allies were already in Paris. We had heard that in secret from the military police who guarded Westerbork. Once in a while, we would have a talk with them. There were some good people among them who would occasionally tell us something. So we thought that it would never get so far, and that it couldn't last much longer. But alas, that wasn't so.

The cars were nailed shut, but you could see the rails through the floor. In a car next to us, and, I think, in our car as well, a few people had brought a saw and other materials in order to escape. I can't remember very well anymore how it was in our car. They did make an attempt, but others called out, "Don't do it." And they stopped. But four people escaped from the car behind us. One of them lost an arm. A woman and a couple of others made it. They landed between the rails, lay there, and then ran into the fields, even though there were SS men on top of the train. But apparently they didn't see it.

The Frank family wasn't in my car. It was an awfully long train. On the way, we tried to look through the slats to see where we were. At one point, someone said that we were passing Katowice. And then he said, "Then, we are going to

178

Auschwitz." And that gave us a terrible scare, because that name was very threatening to us.

And we stopped at a bare platform. The cars were thrown open by men in striped suits. Our baggage, mostly backpacks with clothes and other things, had to be left there. We were told that we would get it back later. But of course we never did. They took the baggage out themselves and we never saw it again.

Everything about our arrival in Auschwitz was so unreal, so beyond reality. It looked like a science fiction movie. I kept on staring. "What is this, actually?" I couldn't comprehend it all. I just kept seeing people, who kept on going around in circles, as if they were on a skating rink, with those terrible yellow lights overhead. I said to a girlfriend who was standing next to me, "What are those people doing there?"

It was night; it was dark.

She said, "Oh Yes, they are running very fast."

"No, they aren't running; they are roller-skating," I said.

But they were people who were running very fast. As a punishment, they had had to run fast around the roll-call place. Even now, I make that association when I go to the Olympiaplein. There is an ice-skating rink there, with the same kind of lights. Then I become so sad: Oh God, there they go again, on those skates. I have had that for a long time.

And then there was the selection, which we didn't understand at all. Actually that was fortunate. There stood Mengele, and he pointed—he didn't say anything; he pointed: To the right, that was us, the young, and in their eyes the healthiest people. The others, the older people and the children, went to the left. We didn't understand what was happening, and I thought, We'll see them again in a little while. While walking on the platform toward Mengele, I was able to speak to my aunt for a minute. And I said to the people in my own group, "We have to stay together." An aunt and an uncle of mine who were getting on in years were there, and a cousin with her

179

three-year-old child in her arms. I never saw them again either.

While we were all standing there in separate groups, men and women mixed together, my uncle came up to me and said, "Do you know where Suze is?"

"I just saw her, but I don't see her now. But I'll go and ask one of the men in striped suits."

Those were Dutchmen who had already been there for a very long time. I asked one of them and got the answer, "They are already dead," as if that were quite natural.

I said, "That isn't possible; I just saw her." I couldn't take it in at all. I thought, that man is not all there. Because he also asked me, "Do you still have any jewelry?" And then I said, "No."

That was something that really hit me. On the way to Auschwitz, the train stopped at one point, the doors were opened, and SS men came inside and asked us if we were still wearing jewelry. I was wearing a small chain ring which I had gotten from my sister, as well as my father's watch, and I had a fountain pen that had been my father's. I said to myself, They won't get these. Nonetheless, they took the little ring off my hand, and I had to give them the watch. I cried terribly over that. Those things were ties to my family. But I threw the fountain pen away, through a crack in the car. Very childish, perhaps, but I thought that the Nazis had no right to my things. Most of the people who still had something had to hand it over. That's why we arrived in Auschwitz with nothing we could turn over.

Later, we stood with our friends, everyone mixed together, and we were told that we had to undress. Now I was a rather prudish girl, so I didn't feel at all happy about undressing. Also, because we had gotten our own clothes back when we left Westerbork. But we had to. And every time they yelled, my friend, Frieda Brommet, who stood next to me, said, "Take something off, now. Those dogs, they'll give you a beating." And then I took off my blouse and skirt. Finally, I got so far that I only had a little undershirt and panties on.

Just like many women there, I was menstruating. I thought—Even if it's crazy—I'm keeping my underpants on. But a Nazi came up to me and said, *"Die Hose nach unten* (take off those pants),″ and I said, ″No!″ He hit me on the head, and then I did take those panties off. I wore a sanitary belt, and he came back to me and tore that belt off. Then I thought, This is the end. I found that so terribly difficult, but I saw that he did the same thing to others. Well, I cannot describe it; how shaken we were.

Next, there were Polish women who were prisoners who tattooed the number on your arm. One would do it very neatly, but another did it in a nasty way—she just made a mess of it, and then a new number had to be put on top, resulting in an inflammation, a swollen arm.

You stood there completely naked. And I still remember the men there stood with their backs to us, since they also had to undress, and they thought it was such an awful spectacle. They ended up someplace else in a building, a sort of tower, with many small windows.

After that we went under the shower. We had to walk behind each other, completely naked, and first dip our feet in this violet water, to be disinfected. They were all such inconsistent things. Afterward, we went to a large area where there were showers everywhere—next to each other and behind each other. We had no inkling of what had happened to other people there, so we simply went, unsuspecting, under those showers. Fortunately, water came out and we could actually wash ourselves.

Then suddenly a German, an SS man, came, with a wooden leg—I will never forget that; he had a stick under his knee. That fellow wasn't in his right mind. He seized a long water hose and started spraying us. He had terrific fun doing that. We were sprayed so hard that we didn't know where to turn. We yelled, ″Hey you, go away!″ because you thought, What could happen next? That man was enjoying it. Finally, he stopped. We were completely soaked, and there wasn't anything to dry off with. Some curtains were hanging there, and we used them to dry ourselves as much as possible.

Then, naked, we went outdoors. It was September, and already the weather wasn't so nice anymore; it was cool. I think that they threw us some clothes then—a dress or something. There weren't any pants. Then, we went to the barracks. That was in Birkenau.

In the barracks, the bunks, one above the other, were in rows. They were cots, but very wide. Seven or eight women had to go in each one. We called it "lined up like spoons." Everyone had to turn around at the same time. You couldn't lie in the position you wanted.

The first night, a woman went outside the barracks; she was shot. That woman, horribly wounded, spent the whole night lying there, groaning. We didn't know what we should do—go out there or not—but the others shouted, "No, no you have to stay in bed; that's not allowed." That woman lay there, dying, in a gruesome way. Then I knew, Yes, they really shoot people here. Early in the morning she was dead, lying in front of the barracks, and we saw that. From then on, I knew for sure that they would shoot people from the towers.

Above all, in the night, when you had to go to the toilet— that is much too nice a word—and you had to cross the *Lagerstrasse* (camp street), you were risking your life. Sometimes the Nazis would see you and would shoot at you. Sometimes nothing happened. So it was always very dangerous.

We were in a very long barracks, with a kind of entryway where we all kept little pots and pans. When we had to stand for roll call early in the morning, we would grab a pan and they would bring a kind of large milk canister, with so-called coffee in it, but it was disgusting. You could ladle some of it out with a cup and drink it. But then five of you, for example, had to drink from that cup. Then we agreed, "Remember—three sips for each person," and then we each had three sips. We stood there watching each other, to be sure that no one took four sips. Then there was some left over. Now everyone could have a fourth sip, because there was still enough.

So the cup went back and forth until it was finished.

I still always count sips, and then my husband says, "God, you're still counting." Yes, but I'm not aware of it; it's very strange.

Anne Frank also stood in the same group with me often, and we used the same little cup and passed it to each other.

It could also happen that someone, in the middle of the night, had a terrible need to go to the toilet, but didn't dare to go outside, and, for God's sake, used one of those little pans. And then, it would be washed out as well as it could be. Already, upon our arrival, we had been warned: "Remember not to drink any water because it is dangerous. You could get typhus." So we didn't do that either. We drank or rinsed our mouths with water as little as possible. There were a lot of rats and so forth. When we could get coffee or tea or whatever it was out of the canister, we rinsed our mouths with it, because you couldn't brush your teeth or anything.

The toilets consisted of huge containers over which a plank was laid, with holes in it. You had to sit on that, rather high up. The Hungarians had the habit of climbing up on it and squatting there on top—something that we Dutch women were never able to pull off. They even sat there, eating their bread. I thought, No, no, that can't be. They were so demoralized and dehumanized that they weren't aware of it anymore. I always walked away from that. I didn't know how to deal with it. It was quite horrifying.

Everything was very unhygenic. I always wondered, why we didn't get sick. But after about fifteen days, I came down with scarlet fever.

There were already people who were quite desperate, who in their despair ran against the wire fences and found death. Their bodies were left lying there as an example for us, so that we would know not to touch the wire—that it was electrified.

Gradually, you began to understand, and there was talk about it, that the people who hadn't come back to us—the older people and the mothers with children—had been gassed. Later, I once asked a *Kapo*—no, it was one of those men in striped suits; they weren't all *Kapos:* "I've heard that the people whom we haven't seen since we got here, died immediately. How is that possible? What happened?" Because I couldn't believe it.

And then he calmly explained to me that those people had gone to the crematorium; that they were gassed, because they were of no value in the work process; that we were going into quarantine because they wanted to keep only the strongest. You didn't want to believe it, but you had to believe it. That was so strange; you felt yourself hurled back and forth.

I shut myself off from everything. When I had to carry rocks over these terrible distances I was apt to say to Frieda, who was walking next to me: "You know, I really enjoyed the concert so much, I heard a lovely concert." She asked, "What is that supposed to mean?" I was far away. My mind was not on the rocks, I didn't feel them no matter how heavy they were. I had shut myself off completely and suppressed all reality. Later on the psychiatrist said, "You had a repression of your consciousness." I did all kinds of strange things without realizing it, some of them very dangerous. But I never thought about it.

An example of this is what happened at selection. I had just come out of the hospital after having scarlet fever, from the *Krätzeblock,* because the doctor, Julika, had said, "If you feel all right now"—I had been there already more than six weeks— "then my best advice to you is to leave the hospital." I did; I walked outside in the rain and immediately went to the showers, and they sprayed me with water. I thought, I can't take it any longer, because I was so weak and I wasn't wearing any clothes. Then I was brought to the Dutch group who had been on the transport with me, to the Dutch people who were already in another barracks. There were Dutch girls and women there whom I knew, and they saw me coming, completely naked. Bloeme Emden came forward; she was wearing a boy's jacket—it was beige, I still remember that—and she took that jacket off and put it on me. That was a blessing. And then they said, "Hey, guys, collect some bread, because she has to have a pair of pants." That jacket came down to my waist. And then they collected bread, and with it they bought a pair of pants for me. That was very, very wonderful.

Afterward, there was a selection. We had a woman doctor from Holland with us, Dr. Knorringa, who watched me closely. She came up to me and said, "I can't believe that you'll make it through the selection, you look so terrible!" I still looked awful. In all that time, I had naturally become very weak, and I had a bad wound on my shoulder—there was a large depression there.

Then Dr. Knorringa said, "Cover your shoulder." After all, you had to walk by Mengele with your arms up. He would pull someone to the side, out of the row, and another would be allowed to go on. Dr. Knorringa came to me and said, "I don't know. Try not to walk by there; because I don't think you have a chance. It would be very risky. You don't look well."

Now there was a little wall, as high and as wide as a table, and the *Aufseherinnen* walked along and whipped anyone who got close to that wall. Actually, I was just standing there, looking, and suddenly I crossed over to the other side—like a flash. I don't think that they saw me go over the wall. On the other side, there was someone sitting at a table who wrote down your number, if you were going on the transport. I remember that I said, with great bravado: "Just like that, I got through it." I hadn't gone through the selection; I probably wouldn't have made it. But something like that, so spontaneous . . . on an impulse, I got through it. It was completely crazy—close your eyes and jump—just like that I went over the wall.

I have already told about how we stood for roll call early in the mornings and shared that dark water—they called it coffee.

Anne often stood next to me and Margot was close by, next

to her or in front of her, depending on how it worked out, because you stood in rows of five. Anne was very calm and quiet and somewhat withdrawn. The fact that they had ended up there had affected her profoundly—that was obvious.

But that was our breakfast. We stood there for hours. You couldn't talk with each other. Once in a while, you would say something on the sly to each other out of the side of your mouth, but that was very risky.

It also happened that, at a certain point, we had to return to one of those huge rooms where we were shaved again. Some of the women ducked it. Then we stood for roll call, and the SS came with dogs and we all had to lift our skirts up, so that they could see who had and who hadn't been shaved. Whoever wasn't shaved would be pulled out and beaten terribly. The next time they didn't try to duck it. That was very unpleasant.

In the beginning, we didn't know the role that Mengele had; we didn't know him. In the first barracks we went to, there were Hungarians as well. They were much more experienced than we. They announced Mengele's arrival: "Here comes the angel of death." That's what he was called. We thought, Oh, those people are exaggerating a bit; it won't be so very special. But, in fact, Mengele came on a regular basis and, every time, selected women for one thing or another, for experiments or, yes, for the gas chamber. We actually didn't realize it fully then, but when I was in the barracks with scarlet fever, I saw much more of him than was to my liking. Then I saw what kind of man he actually was, that the Hungarians were right.

There was a Polish child, a girl about eight years old, who had probably spent her entire life in ghettos and camps. Her parents had already been killed, and we took pity on her. She said, "I know for certain that I am going to the cremma"— that's what we called the crematorium—"because I can't avoid it." She was a very wise child.

"No, we will try to save you," we said.

And the women who served as nurses in the barracks for the sick—generally Polish women who were as tough as nails—

gathered jewelry all over the place, loose stones and so forth that people had in their shoes and where else, I don't know. With their hands full of jewels, they offered them to Mengele if he would just let that child stay alive. But he said, "No, I don't need that." You could find almost anything when you walked down the *Lagerstrasse,* because it was of no value to anyone, only to the Nazis, and all of them already had piles of jewelry. Everyone still tried to buy their lives with gold or jewelry, but that didn't help.

And Mengele put that child on the list. We were all terribly depressed that that little girl, of all people, had to go. He picked her up—that is the insanity that I don't understand; we have talked about that for a long time, wondering how it was possible. He picked her up, kissed her, and put her in a truck. It was a large German army truck, into which all the people went.

Among us were four young Dutch women who were very courageous. I was terribly frightened, but they were so—I could almost say reassuring and courageous. One of them said, "If you speak to my husband, please send him my regards." That man didn't come back either. But the women went off with that incredible courage. And that little girl, too. To the gas chamber, and afterward, to the crematorium. Why? They probably didn't look healthy enough; were a little thin.

———

In the time that Frieda Brommet, the Frank sisters, and I were in the hospital barracks, Mrs. Brommet took care of me and Frieda. Mrs. Frank, likewise, was always near her children, and saw to it that they had something to eat.

Finally, we became so skillful at stealing food that when two girls or women brought soup that wasn't intended for us, we would lie in wait with our little pans. When they came along, we would dip our little pots into the soup, and then we would once again have something to eat. It was some kind of solid food—potatoes or some other stuff.

We all shared with each other. If we didn't have roll call, we were always out stealing food, as much as possible. And while the Frank girls and I were in the sick barracks Mrs. Frank and Mrs. Brommet stole food for us.

Mrs. Brommet dug a hole under the barracks and then she called to me, since I was the first one who had gone into that barracks, and thus the best off as far as health was concerned. I went to the hole and she gave me bread and pieces of meat or sardines from a can stolen from the supply rooms, which were well stocked. In that way, we were always comparatively well fed.

On one of the first days that I was sick with scarlet fever, I soiled my bed while I was asleep. I had terrible diarrhea. I was completely drained. I was so dazed, and I felt so unhappy and helpless. You didn't have any soap or any water. So I asked the others, "Look here, girls, what shall I do now?" But just then an *Aufseherin* came by and commanded, "*Raus, Raus* (Get out, get out)." She showed me a faucet on the wall, and she gave me a small enamel pail in which I had to wash the blanket.

I stood there working for hours, until I thought, Now I'm going to faint, but I didn't. I did sit for a moment under the tap, at the edge of the pail, but she immediately screamed that I had to stand up and keep on working. I spent the entire day rinsing that blanket in that little pail. I also cleaned the mattress. It was a horrible mess. Then I thought, How is it possible that this can happen? That I had to clean all that in such a primitive way. Finally, I finished, and then I had to sleep under the wet blanket. I kept thinking, Oh, now I am going to die, or Now, I'll get pneumonia. But I pushed those thoughts aside right away. And, fortunately, I didn't catch anything. But there were moments, when you were so terribly helpless, because there was no one to help you; they weren't allowed to help you. You just had to see how you could manage by yourself.

———

I was lying on a single narrow cot with Frieda Brommet. She had her head next to my feet. It was impossible to lie next to each other.

————

Upon our arrival, they had cut our hair very short, not bald. But while I was in the sick barracks with scarlet fever, something happened and everyone's heads were shaved bald. Not mine, since I was in the sick barracks. When visitors opened the doors at the back of the sick barracks and called out, "Ronnie, how are you?" I would ask, "Who is it?" Because I didn't recognize anyone anymore with their bald heads. Then they called out their names and I recognized them. Yes, that was weird.

Frieda and I found something in our straw mattress. We were lying on something hard. I picked the mattress apart and then I pulled out a platinum watch—a wonderful thing. I said to Frieda, "Now, we can buy some bread with this." I told Mrs. Brommet and Mrs. Frank about it and pushed the watch out to them through the hole under the barracks, saying, "See what you can get for this." They got a whole loaf of bread—that was really quite tremendous, you know—and a piece of that cheese that stinks—one or another of those cheeses that smell so awful—and a piece of sausage. We had delicious food to eat then, although Frieda wasn't all there most of the time. I fed her small pieces of bread; she was in very bad shape.

When I had to leave the barracks and leave her behind, I thought that I would never see her again, since she was so terribly sick.

Next to us, on the other side, lay a Hungarian girl who was dying in an appalling way. Julika, the doctor, didn't dare to get too close to her since she had typhus and was in a terrible condition—filthy and all curled up. Frieda said, "Oh God, I can't bear to look." And I answered, "Don't look." I looked once in a while, and then I didn't dare to anymore. At a certain point, I heard that it would be over soon. I would gladly have done something for her, but I couldn't. There was a kind of release, and then I saw that she'd died. It was very bad. She lay there for a long time, until a couple of people came who dragged her away. She was simply dumped outside.

There was a Dutch woman lying across from me who had seen me come in. She screamed, "Holland, help, Holland, help!" She had severe typhus. I didn't dare go over to her, but I did call out, "I can't come over to you, and I can't do anything for you, either, but perhaps the doctor can help you." I continued to talk to her. Then it got to the point where, although she was still alive, she was put with all of the people who had died. As she was carried by me on a stretcher, she looked at me and cried, "Holland, help." Well, that was simply awful. Then I just lay there whimpering, but you couldn't do anything. They probably thought, She has, perhaps, only a few hours to live. And they put her outside with the dead.

That is something which is more than loathsome—those dead women lying there for days, until they came and threw them into the carts. The carts which were actually intended for emptying the latrines. They were used to pick up bodies everywhere, and the bodies were just thrown, hup, on top of each other. I always thought that was so dreadful. Actually, I didn't want to see it at all, but I still had to look. I was compelled to look—that was terrible. That was something that was unearthly—you couldn't understand at all that it was real. I saw it on a regular basis—before I went to the sick barracks, and afterward as well.

The Frank girls saw it too. And they experienced precisely what I experienced. They were just as afraid and nervous as I was, and they were apprehensive, just as all of us were. The emotional shock at the existence of something like that—they felt that as well.

The Frank girls had *Krätze,* scabies. Before we landed in the special scabies barracks, there was a selection. Whether they were there or not, I don't know. I think that they had just missed that selection and gone to the *Krätzeblock.*

190

In the *Krätzeblock,* the Frank girls kept very much to themselves. They no longer paid any attention to the others. When
food arrived, they became a bit more animated, and they
shared the food and spoke a little.

During that time, somewhat intuitively—since I thought, It
will keep their spirits up a little—I sang a lot for them. Then
I would be asked, "Hey, Ronnie, sing something else." And I'd
sing well-known songs. That would calm everyone, the Frank
girls too and Nannie Beekman, a very nice girl, and very gentle,
who didn't come back either. There was another girl there,
Coby, whose last name I can't remember. Once, when I sang
a certain song, she said, "Would you sing that song again,
because my husband always used to sing it." I've never sung
it since. I've completely repressed it, so that I don't even remember what song it was. Frieda was there too, and when I
sang for her, very quietly to avoid any danger, a kind of calm-
ness prevailed.

The doctor, Julika—she was a treasure, an angel—she took
care of everything. There was no medicine. Once in a while,
someone would get an aspirin. Or something for dysentery,
charcoal, this *Norit* for people who had very bad diarrhea, but
that was completely useless. It only provided a little consolation. But apart from that, they didn't give us anything. Afterward, there was a selection in our barracks, where there were
only people with scarlet fever and typhus. Such a large number
of them were taken away. There were only, I think, five or six
women and girls left. That evening, Dr. Julika came with a
nurse, and they said, "You all have to be quiet." We also had
to be quiet during the next day, so that they would get the
impression the barracks was empty. In the evening, when it got
dark, we were taken out the back door of our barracks to the
Krätzeblock that was next door. There we went, as it were, into
hiding, and continued to be cared for.

And in this barracks we saw Anne and Margot again. Yes,
and also their mother and Mrs. Brommet, who took care of her
daughter and me there. They wandered all over the barracks,

191

like den mothers in the wild, trying to get as much food for us as possible. It worked.

The Frank girls looked terrible, their hands and bodies covered with spots and sores from the scabies. They applied some salve, but there was not much that they could do. They were in a very bad way; pitiful—that's how I thought of them. There wasn't any clothing. They had taken everything from us. We were all lying there, naked, under some kind of blankets. Two of us shared a blanket, lying in a single cot. They expected more people would come into the barracks. However, it wasn't very full. Of course, they had taken away a lot of people.

The a selection was incomprehensible. At the selection I experienced in the sick barracks, strong women, who were in good shape physically, were nevertheless taken away. We were told that if Mengele were to come, you had to stand in front of him looking as strong and as vigorous as possible. I still looked reasonably well then, I was well fed, I had something in reserve from my days in Westerbork, and I went to stand in front of him. And then you actually stood there thinking, Will I get a cross or a line? Well, I didn't get a cross so I could return to the cot, and the others—they got crosses and had to leave. But there were also girls there, such as Monica Rosenthal, who was as thin as a rail, who came through it. Another woman—the mother of twins who were in hiding in Holland—who was pretty gaunt, was selected. Arbitrariness was the rule.

When there was a selection, then everyone looked to each other for protection. We all stood as close together as possible. The Frank girls were there as well, with their mother, naturally. You didn't know what was going on. But at a certain point, you had to go out and walk by Mengele. You didn't know what your fate would be.

Your fate could be that of a young girl, who knelt on stones, next to the *Lagerstrasse*. We always had to lift her head up as we walked by, and then she'd collapse again, and one or another of the SS men passing by would jab her from above. That child was starving; I don't believe that she got any food or care.

Right next to her, there was a basin with water. I always had the feeling she would end up in that water if she fell over. For days that girl sat there dying. It was an awful sight.

With reference to that, the following happened to me after the war. We were visiting acquaintances who had just moved. They had a large living room, and in front of the window there was a statute in white stone of a kneeling girl. Suddenly I saw it, and I became so terribly upset that I wanted to leave. I thought, I can't look at it anymore.

After we had left, I said to my husband, "I'm never going there again."

He asked, "What's the matter?" and I answered, "That statue they had, it reminds me of the girl in Auschwitz."

He really understood that. and said, "I'll ask whether they'll remove it from the room; otherwise, we won't go there again."

It's very difficult to describe your feelings because they changed all the time since something else was always happening. If you had to walk with the whole group, then it might be that you were walking to the gas chambers—you didn't know. Thus, there was a terrible anxiety. I was always looking to see where I could escape to; it wasn't possible, but I had the idea that it should be possible; but it wasn't.

When I got scarlet fever, they said that I would die because I couldn't be taken into the sick barracks since the Polish nurses there said, "Oh, just put her down outside; she's going to die."

Then, I cried out that I didn't want to die, and the others actually bought me a place in the sick barracks with bread. I even had to give up my dress, which they told me would be returned later, but that wasn't true. They took everything that I still had, and then I was permitted to go into the sick barracks, where it was, nonetheless, very dangerous. They said, "Mengele often comes here and there are selections." I didn't know where to turn then.

Sometimes, I had the feeling that I was just living from one moment to the next; it was so chaotic.

Once, shortly before we went on the transport to Libau, we were terribly frightened—I had already left the *Krätzeblock* by then. In the middle of the night, we were taken to a barracks that was really nicely decorated, with curtains in front of the cots and wonderful colored blankets. We were so frightened and said, "This is our last night, they only want to torment us by letting us sleep in nice beds, with nice blankets." We were so afraid that we didn't dare to close our eyes. Nothing happened.

The following morning, we were simply taken to a barracks from which we would depart, but it was still uncertain whether we would really leave. Then they threw us some clothes and shoes which didn't fit at all. We traded with each other. Afterward, we stood in a row, ready to go, and then a couple of Polish women came who wanted to exchange me for one of their Polish women. They thought, Those Dutch women—they aren't worth anything. We didn't count for anything with the Poles; we were nothing. They began to pull at me and to hit me. They tried to push the woman, whom they ostensibly wanted to save, into the row with us.

I called for help, and a life-and-death battle broke out. Nevertheless, they couldn't get me. The others held onto me so tightly that I was able to stay where I was. They weren't able to seize me, but I was really terribly afraid. I thought, Now, I'll have to go among all of those Poles; I don't even speak their language. They would have murdered me then, or something like that. But it turned out all right.

Afterward on the way to the train there was a large army car, with soldiers standing next to it. I was walking together with Beppie Schellevis, my girlfriend who lives in Hilversum now, and Bep said, "You go on that side of the car, and I'll go on the other side, and then we'll meet in the front, because. . ." We were very close to the car, when one of the men standing there said in Dutch; "Don't be afraid, because you're getting bread and sausage. You are leaving on the train." In fact we did get bread and sausage from him, all of us, and we were really so relieved.

In the meantime on the train I felt such anguish; all sorts of things go through your head: What will I do, what will my mother do—because she had stayed behind, alone—and now, I certainly can't find my father again (but he was no longer alive, which I didn't know then), and other thoughts of that kind flash through your mind. The train took us to Libau.

Part of my salvation was surely that I fought starvation tooth and nail, since I certainly didn't want that. From the very beginning, actually, beginning with the arrival in Auschwitz, I thought, They won't get me, I don't want to die, and I have to get out of here. I always had that feeling, and I was able hang on to that idea. When I saw others who were desperate and who said, "Now, tomorrow, I'm going to the wire," or something like that, then I would still always try—it didn't always work—to talk them out of it. Each human life lost was something I found so horrible that I had to try to save it.

I also found support in the group that had already been formed in the prison on the Weteringschans. A few of them disappeared—I don't know what happened to them. All sorts of groups, naturally, were formed by women who were attracted to one another or who got along better.

Anne and Margot Frank and their mother were also in a group, made up of people they had known from the Annex—although we had no notion of the Annex; we didn't know anything about that. And there were also some Jewish women from Germany who were with them. They probably also got support from each other, although I don't believe the Franks spoke German, you understand.

We already had our own group. A little later, Frieda joined us. Quite casually: "Well, here I am." At first some resented that, since we were all sitting there in sackcloth and ashes, as it were, and she came in a little too cheerfully. Sometimes you react strangely when things are tense, where your life is at risk.

195

Some people can't understand that at all. But I had to laugh, and from that moment, Frieda and I were always together. And Beppie Schellevis as well, who would always make us laugh. That's how it is even today.

In that other camp, in Libau, we weren't together in the same barracks—there were rooms that had forty women in them— and I really began to go downhill. Then, one day, Beppie came to see me, and she said, "You have to see if you can switch so that you can be with us, because you're not doing well here." It worked out. Then we wrote a musical and an operetta, which we all performed. And we had great fun, although we always had someone on the lookout, since it was a small camp, and we didn't want the *Aufseherinnen* to learn about it. Those were some wild moments filled with laughter.

That wasn't the case in Auschwitz. It didn't occur to you to laugh there, no, and certainly not so exuberantly as we later laughed in Libau. In Auschwitz, you kept your mouth shut as much as possible, because you didn't know what kind of a reaction there'd be. In Libau, the regime was much more moderate. In the beginning, the *Aufseherinnen* were very friendly. They asked us what it had been like in Auschwitz, and then we told how terrible it had been for us.

But that only lasted for about a week. Then the *Aufseherinnen* were ordered not to be so nice to us and to hit us. Suddenly they changed. They began screaming, and they had us stand at roll call for hours and hours, sometimes for an entire night. Then they became very harsh with us. But in Auschwitz, fear and threats prevailed continuously; you really had to fight for your life. In Libau, fortunately, that was not the case. Libau was mild compared to Auschwitz.

Because there was a lot of aimless shooting, we had agreed to change places with each other constantly. When we walked in a row of five, and also at the roll call, we saw to it that whoever stood in front would stand in the second row the next day. Those in the back would go up to the front. We always changed places. That way you minimized your risk. If they shot, they usually shot at the first or the last row. That was one way to take into consideration the risks of death, but of course, you didn't have any authority of your own.

No one came to rescue us. Once, some Russian airplanes flew over and dropped pamphlets. There was also a Russian bombardment. I think they hit a soldiers' camp of the SS. We couldn't have wished for anything better. But we ourselves didn't get anything out of it.

In the long run, we became very bitter, since we thought, Why don't they come to help us now, and why can't they attack the camp? Once in a while, we heard something. In Auschwitz, there was a whole underground, and they could get news on the radio, and then that would quickly spread. When it appeared that Roosevelt had said something positive we were all elated. There was a conference, and Churchill said this and that. That heartened us, but in fact, nothing happened.

I had the very strong sense that we were in a place that no one knew of, that nobody knew where to look for us, that they couldn't find us, and that in fact we had been left to our fate.

You could do nothing yourself, say for example, steal a weapon and shoot down the lot. You only had your body, and if you were lucky, you had a dress or a jacket on it—that was all you had.

It was very difficult to imagine that a God existed. We wanted it to be so because we wanted to have something to hold on to. But on the other hand, you couldn't reconcile the fact that if there really was a God, that He would allow life to go on as it did here. That little children and old people were murdered—that has remained a perpetual dilemma for me. And then the brutality all around you. That there could be a God who organized that, or approved of it, or who didn't care—I had a great deal of difficulty with that.

I remember that I was lying once next to our *Stubenälteste* (barracks leader) in Libau, who said to me, "We ought to pray more." I had been brought up completely without religion, so I didn't know how to pray. Then she said, "I'll teach you a

197

prayer." Then we prayed every evening, and that calmed me, with a sense that I had indeed done something. But I don't believe that had anything to do with God, because I was angry with Him. I believe that I still am. I still don't have any answer; I can't, I can't find any peace with that.

In Auschwitz, I met a woman who always—on the Sabbath as well—said her prayers. When there were holidays, she knew. We often had no notion of time, but she knew exactly if it was New Year's or something else, and she said her prayers. On Yom Kippur (the Day of Atonement), she fasted. We said to her, "You don't have to do that because we already don't get enough to eat." But no, she fasted.

She was determined, and she did it with a great deal of dignity, full of respect. She was really a very special woman. She also survived and found her children again. She came from an Orthodox background, and that made a big difference, but I have never been able to handle it.

I had a great deal of difficulty with it. I thought of my grandmother—a healthy, kind person, seventy-seven years old when she was taken out of her house. And then my mind stops—I cannot connect that with God. I don't know how to deal with that. And my nephews and nieces, small children, who were still so young—I don't understand that.

In Auschwitz, it wasn't ever possible to put anything down on paper, but in Libau, I was able to put together a small collection of poems that I wrote there.

You become very resourceful. Because we didn't have any paper, I used the paper that was lying under our straw mattress. It was gray packing paper. We tore pieces of it off. Then, we pulled a thread out of the blanket and made a loop in a piece of steel wire. With that, we pulled the thread through the paper, and we bound a little book. That was a tremendous possession. We found a little pencil in the factory.

In the book, I wrote all of the poems that came up in me. Poems about the uncertainty and the fear and what might be waiting for us. We were there in the mountains—it must be a beautiful winter sports area now—there was a lot of snow, and I would write about what would happen on the other side of those mountains when one day we would really be able to go over there.

We stood at roll call, and we put our pants, which we had washed in the snow, on our backs, so that the sun could dry them. We also stood for entire nights at roll call, so it wasn't always so pleasant. In the barracks, we had a table—an enormous luxury—and a couple of stools, and you could sit at the table writing, or up in your cot. That was a great luxury for us.

Behind the Mountains

I saw the birds in their free flight,
And in my thoughts I flew along,
Briefly soared o'er the barbed fence below
And behind the mountains, until the whistles blew.
They call the roll while I stand motionless and erect.

Then each day, I see the sun set once again,
And in my thoughts I go down with the sun,
Behind the mountains, to my native land
For which I long, and where my mother's hand
Waits for me to come. And I pray for peace.

We were liberated on the eighth of May. We saw *Aufseherinnen* leave on bicycles, but we still had to stand for roll call that morning. Then, we had to return to the barracks. Suddenly the gate opened, and Dutch men, with whom we worked in the factory, came through the gate with a radio, and then we called to them, "Go away, go away. That's not allowed."

But they said, "No, you have been liberated, and the Russians are on the way. Nothing more can happen."

We threw our arms around them and we were completely crazy. We took the radio into the barracks.

The first thing that we heard was an appeal from Theresienstadt. Typhus had broken out there, and they were asking for medical help, medicines, dressings, and every kind of aid as quickly as possible. Later it appeared that the appeal was made by our family doctor, Dr. Diamant, who was a prisoner in Theresienstadt, but who did a great deal there as a doctor.

Then we were convinced that we had been freed. I walked out through the gate, because I had to get out from behind those bars. On the street outside the gate, where people were simply walking along, I walked back and forth, yelling: "Hey, look, I'm walking on the street!" I thought that was so tremendous. Now, that was some experience!

Later the Russian commandant came. He spoke Yiddish with us, which we didn't understand, but the Poles and the Russians did. We had to line up, country by country, and everyone sang the "International" in their own language. That was moving. The Russian commandant shouted, "There won't be another war, and we will always be free." He saw to it that an enormous amount of food was provided.

That was May 8, and we left on May 18, but we actually didn't know where we were or what direction we should take. We just walked at random. We got a cart and a horse, which we simply took from a farmer. At that point, we thought we had the right to do it. We put the people who couldn't walk on the cart.

At some point, we got to the Czechoslovakian border, and it appeared that we could go from there to Prague by train. But I said, "I don't want to go to Prague; I have to go to Amsterdam." I didn't understand how that worked. But we went to Prague, which was the nearest place. That took two days. We stayed in Prague for about three or four weeks. We had nothing. The Dutch government didn't show up, and there was absolutely nothing. No one showed any concern or did anything for us. Then the Belgians and the Swedes took an interest and provided food and beds and shelter.

Many of those in my group, myself included, had gotten

scabies, and five of us had to go into the hospital. There we were scrubbed and polished, and we came out like new. Our clothes and everything else were disinfected. There were large kettles on the street in which everything was disinfected. We got our clothes back and the little book, which I had taken with me. It still smells of disinfectant, after all these years. Odd.

From Prague, we left with a Belgian transport for Pilsen, where we were turned over to the Americans by the Russians. We were brought through Bavaria to Bamberg, in large army trucks. We stayed there for a week, in a very large barracks while they purged the transport of many SS men, Dutch SS men, NSB men who had fled—this, that, and everything.

Very slowly we chugged toward Holland in freight trains— which in and of themselves weren't so nice, but it was handled in a completely different, friendly fashion.

In Maastricht, the Dutch Red Cross was waiting for us with cups of coffee. Some people, without further ado, threw it away, and others said, "Oh, let's drink it, then at least, we can say we've gotten something from the Red Cross."

We had, after all, been completely deserted in a horrifying way. In Prague, I had written a letter to my mother, thinking it would be quickly forwarded by the Red Cross, so that they would know at home that I was still alive. That letter arrived in October 1945, and I came home at the end of July 1945, so the letter, of course, didn't have any meaning anymore. I kept the envelope as a curiosity.

In Prague, they had also told us that it made no sense to go to Holland. According to them, in the Hague, where I had to go, everything had been leveled and no one was alive. We actually stood there, wondering: Shall we stay in Prague, then? What in God's name can we do in Holland, where we don't have anyone anymore. And so we stayed. That actually happened. Later, we heard from others that it wasn't true and that only Bezuidenhout had been bombarded in the Hague. My mother lived nearby, and I thought, Let's go and look at Holland, and if there really isn't anyone left, we can always go back to Prague. Idiotic thought, but we weren't in any state to think normally. That was very strange.

The reception in the Netherlands was quite wonderful. We were first in Vlodrop, in Limburg, in a cloister, where we were all examined, X-rayed, and so forth. That happened terribly quickly, and then we were taken from there to Eindhoven by car. There I landed in an emergency hospital, set up by Philips, since I had a very high fever. I was in the typhus section, but I said, "I don't have typhus."

Our group was going to continue on, and then I said, "I'm going with you." I asked one of my friends, "Will you see if you can get my clothes, because I'm simply going to walk out of here."

They asked the doctor on duty, who said, "She certainly cannot be moved because she has such a high fever. I can't vouch for anything."

To which I said, "Oh, that man is not all there. I don't have typhus. I'm getting dressed, and I'm going with you." I wore a pair of SS pants, a blouse, wooden shoes. That was all that I had. On the way, I got another terrible fever. But the closer I got to the Hague, the better I felt.

In Den Bosch, we got half loaves of bread, with a piece of breakfast cake. We ate everything that came along—we were starving. From Den Bosch, we went to Rotterdam by boat, and from there, by train, to the Hague.

Those friends of mine, who had worked in KIFO (the photo shop in the Hague), and who had been with us in the resistance, lived in Spoorwijk. We went there by train, and since the train kept stopping, I said, "Guys, I'm going to go to Rie first for a minute, because I want to know where my mother is." And I got out, thinking, I'll go down along the train embankment.

At the same moment, I was seized by two men.

"Hey, you want to escape? Where are you going?"

I said, "I have to go to the Van Vlotenstraat, number nine."

And they said, "Yes, but you are probably a member of the NSB (the Dutch Nazi organization), trying to escape."

I really had such a hard time convincing them that I had been in a camp. After I had finally made it clear to them, they took me on the back of a bicycle to the train station. But the train had already left for Amsterdam.

There was a policeman there who said, "Here is a paper to fill out for ration cards, and here is this and that." So I took all that and went to sit down on a bench, because I didn't know where else to go.

The policeman said, "Shouldn't you be going home?"

I said, "Yes, but I don't know whether my house is still standing.

"Where is it?" he asked.

I gave him the address, and he gave me some good advice. "Go to number 4, Pletterijstraat. Those are friends of my parents, and they'll be able to tell you whether your mother is there."

And in fact those people picked up my mother, who lived just on the other side of the street, and now . . . that was so marvelous. I looked terrible, but my mother, yes, she had gone to stand at the station every evening, and just this particular evening, she hadn't gone there; she had begun to lose hope because we returned rather late.

Well, that was completely crazy, seeing my mother again. I didn't have any money with me, but I wanted so much to give that policeman something. I did have packs of Lucky Strikes. I gave him a pack of Lucky Strikes and that man was so happy with it.

Then he said, "Do you know how much this is worth?"

"I don't know, but it doesn't make any difference to me," I said, feeling very generous.

I went home with my mother, and we sat up the whole night, talking. I still remember that very well. My mother kept on saying, "Oh, child, how is it possible, how can this be?" I told

her all kinds of crazy things, which we laughed about. That's
how I came home.

How can I find tranquillity,
Years later, the tumult of the men resounds,
The swishing of their whips,
Above the people being pushed along,
And stamping of boots,
Cries of anguish.
I have seen so many go to a desperate death,
Across a dirt path, on which their weakened feet
Dragged them to the gate.
Smoke cannot speak,
From the chimneys, they slip out, formless, above
my head,
And are taken by the wind,
Robbed of their bones.
Since then, despite my clothes, I am naked,
And remain exposed to synonyms.
Therefore, it is not tranquil within,
The whips are still lashing,
And at the most unexpected times,
The packing paper pictures come forth,
Chilly, yellowed, gray from smoke,
And stiff with death, at night, when I want to sleep.

About the Author

WILLY LINDWER, Dutch filmmaker and son of Jewish parents who survived the German occupation in hiding, was born in 1946 in Amsterdam. He has produced numerous documentaries for Dutch television and as part of international co-productions. His documentary about the last seven months of Anne Frank was first shown on Public Television to mark the sixtieth anniversary of Anne Frank's birth and won an international Emmy Award.